CROSS THAT BRIDGE

The Effective Guide
to Achieving Your Goals and
Living a Purposeful Life

Samuel J. Lucas

DISCLAIMER

The advice provided in this material is general advice only. It has been prepared without taking into account your objectives, financial situation, or needs. Before acting on this advice you should consider the appropriateness of the advice, having regard to your own objectives, financial situation, and needs. Where quoted, past performance is not indicative of future performance.

The author and the publisher of this book disclaims all and any guarantees, undertakings warranties, expressed or implied, and shall not be liable for any loss or damage whatsoever (including human or computer error, negligent or otherwise, or incidental or consequential loss or damage) arising out of or in connection with any use or reliance on the information or advice on this site. The user must accept sole responsibility associated with the use of this material, irrespective of the purpose for which such use or results are applied. The information in this material is no substitute for financial advice.

© **Copyright 2020 - All rights reserved.**

This document is geared towards providing exact and reliable information in regard to the topic and issue covered. The publication is sold with the idea that the publisher is not required to render accounting, officially permitted, or otherwise, qualified services. If advice is necessary, legal, or professional, a practiced individual in the profession should be ordered.

From a Declaration of Principles which was accepted and approved equally by a Committee of the American Bar Association and a Committee of Publishers and Associations.

In no way is it legal to reproduce, duplicate, or transmit any part of this document in either electronic means or in printed format. Recording of this publication is strictly prohibited and any storage of this document is not allowed unless with written permission from the publisher. All rights reserved.

The information provided herein is stated to be truthful and consistent, in that any liability, in terms of inattention or otherwise, by any usage or abuse of any policies, processes, or directions contained within is the solitary and utter responsibility of the recipient reader. Under no circumstances will any legal responsibility or blame be held against the publisher for any reparation, damages, or monetary loss due to the information herein, either directly or indirectly.

Respective authors own all copyrights not held by the publisher.

The information herein is offered for informational purposes solely and is universal as so. The presentation of the information is without a contract or any type of guarantee assurance.

The trademarks that are used are without any consent, and the publication of the trademark is without permission or backing by the trademark owner. All trademarks and brands within this book are for clarifying purposes only and are owned by the owners themselves, not affiliated with this document.

CONTENTS

Introduction

Envision the end from the beginning   1

Sharpen your saw   6

Successful people rate very high in self-awareness   7

Self-confidence will make you achieve whatever you put your mind to 15

It starts with your mindset   27

Develop the right attitude for success   32

Failure is a necessary ingredient to achieve success   33

Self-limiting beliefs are barriers between you and your goals   38

Your problems are guidelines to something greater   44

Never take your time for granted   49

Do whatever you can do, right this moment!   56

Let's achieve your goals   66

Do the most important things first!   67

You must set realistic goals in order to achieve them   74

The Path to Achieving Your Goals   82

Everything start with a decision   83

You have to be flexible to navigate life successfully   89

You must reduce your stress level to be able to achieve your goals	95
The part of life you neglect will return with its consequences	100
You can't do more than what you've prepared you body for	108
The only time you have is now	112
Final Thoughts	119

INTRODUCTION

INTRODUCTION

"If you want to reach a goal, you must see the reaching in your mind before you actually arrive at your goals."
Zig Ziglar

ENVISION THE END FROM THE BEGINNING

Before, or at the beginning of this year, a lot of us took out a piece of paper, and thought about what we didn't achieve last year, and what we would like to achieve this year. We scribbled these ambitions on the paper and tag them our new *New Year's resolution*. Great! This list has, over the years made us hopeful along the year, and enabled us to see a flashing light at the end of the tunnel-- which in itself-- is a good thing.

However, it worthy of note that not everybody knows the difference between a goal and a resolution. It is also cogent to note that only a few understand how they can properly set and achieve their goals. The statistics by the Brain Research Institute pointed out that only 9.2% of all people ever feel that they are successful in achieving their New Year's resolution, while 42% give up after the first month.

So, if you are looking for a way to achieve some level of improvement, and save some money this year, there is a way out. Your New Year's resolution can be transformed into achievable goals if you would be diligent with the recommended tips, strategies, and suggestions offered in this book.

More so, setting goals, and having ambition is a huge part of our identity, so it is advisable not to take it lightly. It starts with a decision to achieve your goals before you are able to envision yourself clearly at the destination you would like to see yourself, coupled with having the right mindset; whether your heart is set for skydiving, getting your dream job, starting a business, etc.

Further, have you ever sat down to think about what you will be doing in the next five years? Do you already have a clear picture of your main objectives? have you thought about what you would like to achieve by the end of today? All these are also parts of important aspects of setting life goals.

It goes without saying that you need to set goals if you want to succeed because you will lack direction and focus if you fail to set goals. In addition to providing you with a benchmark for determining whether you are actually succeeding or not, goal settings also allow you to take control of your life's direction. Check this out: having 100 million dollars in your account is solid evidence of success if your goal is to become rich. However, if your goal is to get involved in charity, then keeping the money may not count as what you will define as success.

For you to be able to accomplish your goals, you, therefore, need to first start with the end in mind, the way Stephen Covey has put, and practice everything recommended tips herein to achieve your goal.

INTRODUCTION

Therefore, setting your goal commences with making the decision to be successful, seeing the reaching in your mind before you actually arrive at your goals, careful considerations, and determination of how it would be achieved. You will also need to be hardworking for you to be able to achieve your goals. Many and many of such tips have been discussed in this book. All you have to do is just follow the guides, and you will see yourself leading a successful life.

Actionable Advice

★ You need to make up your mind that you are ready to give whatever it takes in achieving your goals.

★ Having a clear picture of your goal in mind is very crucial to achieving your goals.

★ Research has shown that only a few people achieve their new year's resolution, it is, therefore, better to consider your resolutions as a goal.

★ Life will be boring and monotonous without setting goals and ambition, which is a huge part of our identity and existence.

★ You can't be lazy and achieve your goals. You will have to be hardworking, and ready to give whatever it takes for you to be able to get whatever you want out of life.

INTRODUCTION

SHARPEN YOUR SAW

"Your vision will become clear only when you look into your own heart. Who looks outside, dreams; who looks inside, awakes."
C.G Jung

SUCCESSFUL PEOPLE RATE VERY HIGH IN SELF-AWARENESS

Today, when we are always stressed, either from school, work, or other engagements, and it is understandable that we react passively to our immediate environment, thereby overlooking opportunities. Self-awareness is a particularly important skill that we must all acquire to help us progress and improve in the journey of self-development. Self-awareness is how we are able to monitor and evaluate both our internal and external world. Acquiring emotional intelligence and the ability to regulate these emotions is one of the most treasured skills, nowadays; and self-awareness is the cornerstone of that intelligence.

Those who are self-aware have a good understanding of their inner experience and their direct or indirect impact on the external experience of others. Our feelings and thoughts come from signals, either outside or inside of us. Self-awareness has made it possible for us to no longer be knocked down by these signals, but rather to respond to them thoughtfully and objectively.

As the level of your empathy and compassion rises, so does your self-esteem rise. Armed with good intentions and purpose, someone who is self-aware can meaningfully impact their world. Those who are self-aware exhibit self-confidence, self-worth, and have a high level of success rate.

The journey to developing self-awareness is not easy, because it requires high-level cognitive processing. It requires you to be able to gather a lot of information from a different perspective. An objective or open observation of sense, actions, feelings, and desire can catapult you into a flourishing experience. You need not relieve negative emotions, but instead, acknowledge them and learn from their presence. The outcome of this result increases your flexibility and adaptability. Self-awareness also builds resilience, as well as improves your ability to empathize with others.

How Self Awareness Contribute to Building Positive Habit

Your self-awareness usually serves as the guiding light of your thoughts and emotions. It makes you take responsibility for your actions, in order to make the necessary adjustments to achieve the desired outcome. This may sometimes include changing your personality, emotions, or behavior. If this is not achieved, you may find it difficult to make changes to the direction your life is going.

You need self-awareness, for you to take control of your life, create what you desire, and own the future. Where you choose to focus your energy, personality, reactions, and emotions determine your destination in life.

How to Develop Yourself Awareness

1. Ask a Trusted Friend to Describe You

This is necessary because you need someone that will be as honest as possible with you when telling you about yourself. If you don't ask for feedback, especially from those you trust, you can't know what other people think of you. Do you have a mentor? Great! A trusted friend? Awesome! Let them know that you need their sincere feedback to help you and understand grow. You can go further by telling your friend to let you know when you do something you promised to change. For instance, if you know you like interrupting people while they speak, have your friend let you know that you are falling back on your promise. Also, if you feel you need to ask questions to clarify the topics they bring up, please do.

2. Ask for Feedback at Work

This is called 360-degree self-evaluation, that is, an evaluation of both your personal and professional life. Go ahead and develop one, if your organization does not already have this in place.

In addition to asking for feedback from your family and friends, getting feedback from a formal setting is a good idea. Opinions from work open you up to your strength and weaknesses. So, it is important that you write them down as your major take- away. It takes time to develop your self-awareness. Sometimes, it can even take years. However, putting in the necessary effort to be more self-aware can positively improve every aspect of your life, especially your interpersonal and intrapersonal relationships. Take note of any surprising strengths and weaknesses you are unaware that you possess.

3. Take Personality and Psychometric Tests

One easiest way to launch your journey into self-awareness is to take an online test. There are a lot of online platforms that offer the service for free. Although, the results you get might not be accurate, but it will compel you into thinking about the traits you can be closely identified with.

4. Practice Meditation and Other Mindful Habits

A lot of meditations focus on breathing. Meditation is one of the most effective ways of improving the awareness of the mind. You may consider thinking about these questions when meditating:

- How can I improve my success rate?

- What is my goal?

- What am I doing that is hindering my success?

- What am I doing that works for me?

Tasks like jogging, washing dishes, going to your religious house, are typical examples of some of the most regular meditation you practice unknowingly that comes from the daily task that gives you a sense of calmness and allows you to sustain your attention on the present moment.

5. Reflect Everyday

Following this practice religiously will definitely make you improve. All you need to do is to set aside some time at the end of your day, to honestly examine yourself in your personal and professional life. Daily self-reflection is a prerequisite for developing self-awareness. Self-reflection is amazingly effective when it is written down in your journal.

6. Get a Journal

Even if it is not related to your goals, you can write it in your journal. Spare some time every night to write down your feelings, thoughts, failures, and successes of the day. When you record your thoughts on paper, your mind gets relieved of those ideas and clears them to allow for fresh ideas and information. This is to help you grow, track, and move forward in your achievements.

Take out some time to think about the personality you reflect as a leader, and how your employees are likely to view you, in the course of your reflection. Write down your values and what is most important to you at the moment. Think about how you can help others, and further think about how you can do more. The answers you provide to these questions will help you in getting a good grasp on who you are and what you really want out of life.

7. Be Objective with Yourself

Seeing yourself the way you really are can be a daunting process and task, knowing yourself can be an extremely rewarding experience if you invest the right effort. You can then learn to embrace your true self and consequently find ways to improve yourself in the future, if you are able to see yourself objectively:

So, how do you go about this?

- The main idea of this exercise is to have an idea of what makes you unique, and not to compare yourself with others. You need to write down how you see yourself in the world. This can be writing down things you think you are good at, and things you need to improve upon.

- Write down the things you are proud of, including something outstanding you have achieved throughout your life.

- Tell your friends and family to be honest with you about their perception of you and how they feel about you.

- Flashback to your childhood memories and try to recall what usually made you happy back then, and if it has remained the same. If not, what are the reasons?

You will discover new a perspective about yourself and your life, at the end of this simple exercise.

Self-awareness plays an important role in the understanding of ourselves and how we relate to the world outside us. As previously said, it is not easy to develop this level of introspection. You will be able to critically evaluate yourself and your place in people's life when you are self-aware. Surprisingly, a lot of people fear being honest with themselves about their current strengths, problems/challenges, and weakness. However, if you follow the above-mentioned self-aware recommendation, it will skyrocket your level of self-awareness and increase your chances of attaining your goals.

To improve your level of self-awareness, here are some exercises you could consider:

- Observing others

- Having a personal vision

- Doing a Strength Assessment, such as the Values in Action Strength Test from the University of Pennsylvania

- Tai Chi, Qigong, or Yoga

- Practicing mindfulness meditation

Ask yourself these questions to further deepen your self-awareness:

- What does my ideal look like?

- Is there a reason these goals or dreams are important? If so, why?

- Is there anything preventing me from these goals or dreams?

- On the grade of 5-10, how will I rank the most important things in my life: love, relationship, family, money, etc.

- How much time do I dedicate to doing these things?

- What would I recommend to my children to do?

Self-awareness on personality

- How would I describe myself in three words?

- Has my personality changed since childhood?

- What quality do I admire most about myself?

- What is my biggest weakness?

- What am I scared of?

- Do I make decisions intuitively or logically?

After answering these questions, they should give you a lead to having a full grasp of yourself better.

Actionable Advice

★ You need self-awareness to know and understand yourself, and others.

★ Self-awareness will enable you to adequately respond to challenges you may encounter on the journey to achieving your goal.

★ Increased self-awareness will lead to increased self-esteem, which consequently brings out an increased success rate.

★ Self-awareness makes you take responsibility for your actions so that you can make the necessary adjustments to achieve your envisioned outcome.

★ If you want to take control of your life, you need self-awareness, as well as to create what you desire, and own the future you want to see.

"Successful people often exude confidence-- it's obvious that they believe in themselves and what they are doing. It isn't their success that makes them confident, however. The confidence was there first."
Travis Bradberry

SELF-CONFIDENCE WILL MAKE YOU ACHIEVE WHATEVER YOU PUT YOUR MIND TO

Developing Your Self Confidence

If you want to achieve your goals and objectives, you absolutely must have enough self-confidence to see the job through. Because your level of self-confidence must grow to match your goals and ambition as the size grows. Henry Ford said, 'Whether you believe that you can or you believe that you cannot; you are right.' Self-confidence is important. The biggest factor in determining your level of success is usually your self-confidence. Honestly, when you fail to achieve your objectives, it is easy to believe that you do not have the ability, or you are not good enough. But the difference between failure and success is rarely due to any lasting ability. You may lack the whole necessary skills to carry out a task at a very moment, but you can learn everything that is required to know for the task later.

People with self-confidence invite trust and inspire confidence in others. Self-confident people seem at ease with themselves and their works. And every person admires a self-confident person. Some may even envy them a little.

What is self-confidence and its importance?

Regardless of any imperfections or of what others may think about you, self-confidence is understanding that you trust your abilities and that you value yourself and feel worthy.

But self-confidence is at times used interchangeably with self-efficacy and self-esteem. One thing is that don't twist them, they are subtly different.

Self-efficacy is a type of confidence that leads people to accept difficult challenges and keep going in the face of setbacks. When you see yourself, and others like you, mastering skills and achieving goals, you gain a sense of self-efficacy or it sets in. It encourages you to believe that if you learn and work hard in a particular field, you'll succeed. While self-esteem is more of a general sense that you can cope with what's going on in your life. And that you have a right to be happy.

Self-esteem can also come in part from the feeling that the people around you approve of you. So, if you experience a lot of criticism or rejection from other people, you may or may not be able to control this. And your self-esteem could easily suffer except you find some other ways to support it.

It requires effort to be self-confident

You have probably ever once seated down, asked yourself, or wonder what's the secret behind the confidence someone you know exudes and the reason why the person is so positive about herself or himself. It's nothing, but self-confidence. It does not happen by accident. You could be that confident too.

If you continue with positive habits and with the right commitment and effort, your self-confidence will continue growing and build within a short time. It comes from repeated practice and small successes which build into large successes.

Self-confidence may seem to have come naturally to some people, but it is more likely that they had confident role models in their life, from whom they learned or acquired the appropriate confidence building behaviors. It's not some sort of gift that you are born with, you acquire it.

People you find as though they are naturally confident imitated the behavior they saw from their role models. You'll be taking giant strides to build your self-confidence by practicing these same actions.

If other people put you down or if you're naturally self-critical, it's not always easy to be confident in yourself. There are steps that you can take to maintain and increase your self-confidence:

Confidently present yourself

When you lounge around at home with family or friends, you may be unkempt because they know who you are, and your appearance is unlikely to have a huge bearing on their thoughts about you.

But take time to ensure that you are well-groomed and wearing clean, well-fitting, and appropriate clothing if you have an important event e.g., business meeting or an interview. It will give you that extra boost of confidence. How you feel about yourself is reflected in your appearance.

You feel great about yourself when you know you look great. As you notice the difference, that little effort goes a long way because it will bring a new approach into more areas of your life.

You may be more concerned about the quality of your work than your appearance if you're the type who works from home. You may often work with casual cloth but when you have something so challenging to do, dress smartly, prepared, and focused on the challenge ahead.

It isn't that you are trying to impress but to give yourself a little bit of a confidence boost. It's as though telling the challenge ahead that you know you'll be tested, but you are going to get the best you have and, you know you can beat it.

The real benefit of appearing well is what you are communicating to yourself. People often think that dressing better is about impressing others. Though for some people it may be.

Smile and look at people in the eye

So many people do not smile when they meet other people. It also sounds obvious to state that when you smile, you become more confident and feel happier. A smile will help you build a good rapport with others.

As you start to interact better with others, your self-confidence grows until communicating with ease becomes a natural process. And improving the quality of your interactions enables others to feel more at ease in your presence. Because it shows that you have a certain ease and warmth about you when you smile and make eye contact.

Greeting people with a warm, sincere smile and gentle eye contact is an assertive behavior that benefits both parties and helps build confidence for both as your behavior will be showing them that you are trustworthy. And telling them that you come in peace. You pose no threat to them.

A simple smile and some eye contact can open doors to people you just met. But if you don't smile and, you don't make eye contact, you are not signaling to others that you are open to communication and connection. Though some people want to, they fear rejection that's why they won't. And many of those who lack self-confidence are fearful of reaching out and connecting with others. So, your self-confidence is something that must be built.

Giving genuine compliments to others

It becomes easier for you to find the positives in others that you would like to compliment, but it may take a little time at first. The compliments should always be honest and genuine. Don't mistake this approach for insincere flattery. It demonstrates that you feel good enough about yourself to give positive feedback to others when you take the time to compliment others.

Your self-confidence grows because of that. And you realize that your life is in better shape than you may have previously thought as you do so. Not only will you find positives in others, but you will start to see more positives in every area of your life too by adopting the necessary mindset.

One great thing about love is that you experience it yourself when you give it. Think about how you feel when you compliment or help someone you genuinely care for. You'll discover that you always feel good yourself. Sincerely complimenting others is one of the simplest but purest forms of love.

This has a powerful impact on your self-confidence. The very act of searching for the positives in others makes you feel better and trains you to see the positives in life. As it passes through you, you must experience it for yourself. Your gift to others is also a gift to yourself. Those little acts of love, or if you prefer to call it kindness, that come from within you, must pass through you before it passes to the other person.

The practice of appreciation

When you appreciate the positive things in your life, you take a moment to focus on how your life is better because of those things, but you don't just identify the things that you like. Though they are there, you won't easily identify them always. Because, sadly, humans find it incredibly easy to find the negative in their lives.

By doing so, you only want to develop a more realistically optimistic view whereby you can identify and appreciate the positives in your life. And are not trying to develop delusions about how amazing and wonderful your life is. When you practice the act of appreciation each day, you will eliminate negativity from your life.

All you only need is to start seeing the good in your life and appreciate it. You don't always have to improve your life to be happier with it and have more self-confidence. You discover that your life is better than you normally think it is, and that is important. You begin to feel some real joy when you take some time to appreciate the good things in your life.

Stick and play to your strengths

You are likely going to struggle, and your self-confidence will be impacted if you spend a lot of your time performing tasks that you are not best suited to perform. Because throughout your lifetime you will encounter tasks you can't perform well. But it's nothing to be embarrassed about; it's the same for everybody. Everyone can do most things but what differs is the standard to which each person can perform the task.

Delegate or outsource the tasks which do not suit your strengths where possible. Make sure the work you sought is in an area that makes the most of your knowledge, strengths, and skill set. You'll feel like an expert and know without a doubt that you excel in that area. So, you must know your strengths and play to them. You will be better able to perform the task and your self-confidence will receive a boost with each task that you complete. Instead, focus on doing whatever you're best at, not what you're not.

You do not need to waste your time being any more than competent if the task doesn't lie in one of your strengths. And that's fine. Though there are a lot of things that do not fall within your strengths, you do need to be competent at them.

For self-confidence in life, it is far better to keep building on your strengths and you don't have to be great at everything. The only exception to this should be for things you genuinely love doing.

Accept your imperfections

Nobody has ever been perfect, and nobody will ever be. You can always try doing your best rather than seek to achieve perfection. You can strive to do better next time around and learn from the experience. Perfection is neither a possibility nor a necessity. It's just a mechanism used to inflict pain upon yourself.

Be it at a skill, a personal trait, a project, a product, get feedback from other people, from results, or the world at large. As you review the feedback, you will identify any improvements you need to make. The feedback loop allows you to continuously improve in whatever you do. And the key thing to remember is that once something is done, it can always be improved.

You can never get feedback as there is nothing to improve you if you never even start what you intend to do. If you wait for perfection before you take action, you will never begin. That's why being done is better than perfection.

Imperfections only show that you're human because nobody is. It isn't that there is something wrong with you. As long as you are willing to take action, receive feedback, and make improvements and you will continually make progress. And this way, without the stress-inducing pressure of always trying to be perfect, you will constantly improve. So, wherever you are is fine.

Get yourself prepared

Practice allows you to reduce the fear associated with stepping into the unknown, especially if it's a presentation. It allows you to familiarize yourself with the challenges that lie ahead.

You've practiced in advance to perform whatever needs to be done. Your self-confidence grows as you practice, and you also realize that you are capable of dealing with the challenge.

Have some notes on standby to jog your memory in case you are concerned about something going wrong. Identify your worst fear, for example, if you forget your speech. Prepare ahead, identify where your problem lies, and proffer solutions to it.

You can implement your solution whereby you forget your words. This will give you the self-confidence to believe that you can cope with whatever goes wrong.

Set goals and work to achieve them

You can see the progress that you are making towards fulfilling your purpose as you achieve your goals. As you see that you can achieve whatever you want from life with the accomplishment of each goal, your self-confidence receives a little boost. Also, you can focus better, and each day has meaning. You know where you're going and what you are trying to achieve when your life has direction and purpose. Set goals that will help you to consistently work towards these objectives.

It may only be a tiny improvement each day, but you won't believe the difference as your self-confidence will have soared in some months. When you set goals effectively you realize that every day is about stepping in the right direction. And a small step in the right direction is something which should be celebrated. Also, the continuous achievement of goals is progress, no matter how small that goal may be. Self-Confidence starts growing daily as you realize the achievements too.

Embrace anything you love doing

Love comes in many forms and when you make room for love in your life, you will be happier and more confident. Love is the most powerful emotion. But sadly, we only tend to think of love in terms of that poppycock that Hollywood movies show us.

Creating rooms for things you love in your life is one of the most pivotal things you can do. Sadly, one of the first things you cut tends to be your favorite hobbies when you struggle with time creation. Nonetheless, the hobbies you love replenish you with positivity which assists to increase your happiness and health. That also makes you feel more in control of your life and increases your self-confidence.

Taking time to find out where you should be spending more of your time makes you feel happy and blessed. Similarly, it's a way of caring for yourself. And caring for yourself will always boost your self-confidence.

There'll always be things that you ought to do which you don't love. But you can love something about them. For example, you can take some of your time to mull over the wonderful things you enjoyed from public services that are being rendered to you when paying your taxes. You can prevent them from damaging your happiness and self-confidence by finding positives in these types of situations which you normally view in them a negative light.

Always try to do your best

Always try to give your best in whatever you do because it also helps you in building a reputation with friends, family, colleagues, and customers which enables you to receive positive, self-confidence-building feedback. You know you could not have given anymore when you know you have given your absolute best to a task. Because it allows you to feel relaxed and more confident about your performance. You can strive to do your best no matter what kind of work you do.

Continuous improvement ensures that your self-confidence is regularly reinforced. You will realize that your best continues to get better each time. A lot of people usually think they need to have confidence before they can commit themselves fully to everything they do. And thinking that way is as though putting the cart before the horse. All you need is to only give your best effort each time and learn from your outcomes.

Accept rejection and disapproval

You end up sacrificing your own goals, dreams, and aspirations when you value the approval of others too high, which is a form of self-rejection. And this form of self-rejection has disastrous consequences for your self-confidence. Know well that there will always be people who disapprove of you no matter what you do in life. You could bend over backward to try and please them but even if you succeed, it would be the person you are pretending to be. It wouldn't be you they are approving of.

Prove to yourself instead of proving to others that you are competent and confident, and others will see it anyway. And they are rarely worth worrying about if they don't see it. You'll be free of feeling compelled to impress people when you give up the need for approval. Instead, you'll become more authentic and real with yourself.

Start improving your self-confidence today and begin living as the person you long to be. Because your faith in yourself will grow with every small step you take. Why not select one of the listed ways of improving your self-confidence and start working on it today? You should know that you owe it to yourself to develop your self-confidence. Because you will be wondering why you didn't take action sooner by the time you start. Though implementing the listed ways may not be able to boost or cure the problem of all your self-confidence but it will take your self-confidence to a whole new level. You will be happier, healthier, and more motivated to challenge yourself to be the best that you can be with your new-found confidence. While some people make it look easy and natural, their high self-confidence is a result of learned behaviors. You too can learn these behaviors and experience the many benefits of high self-confidence. Building your self-confidence takes time, focus, and effort. It is not a magic trick.

Actionable Advice

★ You need self-confidence to be able to achieve your goal.

★ Your self-confidence must be able to match the size of your goal.

★ You will inspire others to attain success when you have self-confidence.

★ Self-confidence is understanding that you trust your abilities and that you value yourself and feel worthy of what you want to achieve.

★ It takes consistency in practice to be self-confident.

"When you master your mind and your deep unconscious abilities, you will move ahead faster and achieve more in a shorter period of time than perhaps you could even imagine today."
Brain Tracy

IT STARTS WITH YOUR MINDSET

Develop a Success-Friendly Mindset

A success-friendly mindset helps to strengthens your confidence level and enable you to make smarter decisions that will lead to a better personal and professional result. A person who lacks a success friendly mindset or is pessimistic will usually not excel in their activities. Success friendly mindset is very integral to building and maintaining confidence. If you possess a pessimistic mindset, it will become difficult for you to motivate others to be close to you.

Some of the strategies that help you develop a success-friendly mindset are provided here:

Don't just stay in one position: One of the things that will help you develop a positive mindset, and also help you boost your confidence is to avoid remaining in one spot. An important ingredient of growth is to keep moving. If at any point, you feel like you are not moving or learning new things, then you haven't made the effort to move and experiment and experience new things. You will subconsciously begin to acquire a positive mindset in life, and you'll begin to develop faith in yourself when you can recognize your growth. One sure way to avoid stagnation is to build a network of talented colleagues and mentors and to develop a daily routine that enables you to monitor your progress.

Set definite and achievable goals: You will develop a winning mindset by setting achievable goals and deliberately setting a time frame for each. A lot of people rely on New Year's resolutions, but the truth is that more than 90 percent of New Year's resolutions fail. So instead of allowing your inability to accomplish your new year resolutions to affect your confidence level, it is better to set a realistic goal within a specific time frame, which is feasible from the outset. You would realize that your confidence level will increase once you can achieve those time-bound goals consistently.

Learn from your failures: The fact that this point is repeated shows how important it is to learn from one's mistake. All winners have at one point or the other in their life experience losing. Don't let your losses weaken your mindset. Failure should be considered an opportunity to learn. When you develop a positive mindset towards failure, it helps you less susceptible to anxiety and you begin to develop a winning mindset.

Many people who succeed too often do not challenge themselves to the next level. So, if you fail at a thing, there are chances that you have grown beyond your previous level.

Try to be conscious of your growth: Nothing improves a person's growth than understanding how much such a person has evolved and grown. People with a winning mindset are very deliberate about growth. You must put deliberate effort into developing yourself and growing. People who have experienced different levels of growth are typically happy to take on new challenges and have a strong conviction in their ability to surmount such new challenges.

Trust your instinct: You must learn to trust your instinct to develop a winning mentality that will boost your confidence. According to many studies, trusting our instinct can enable us to make smart decisions. While it is important to conduct research and do some fact findings, in certain spontaneous instances, it is important that you trust your guts and instinct to make good and firm decisions. You must be the number one believer in yourself. If you successfully do this over time, it will increase your confidence level.

Life will present you with different scenarios that will require on spot response from you, your winning mindset will empower you to make such on the spot decisions without a doubt.

Avoid competing with other people: Although, it is important to look up to those who have accomplished feats that you hope to attain, however it is equally essential that you don't put yourself in competition with them because such unhealthy competition may lead you to develop some complex that would make you feel like a failure. Compete only with yourself and draw inspiration from other achievements. You should measure success based on your benchmark and not on the success of others. Consider their achievement as a template that will help you navigate a similar path without making the same mistakes your role models have made in the past.

Actionable Advice

★ Having a success-mind set helps to reinforce your confidence to be able to make wise decisions.

★ Be committed to life-long learning, which will open your mind to possibilities.

★ Set achievable goals and have a time frame you wish to achieve the goal.

★ Consider failure as an opportunity to learn. Don't allow your losses to weaken your mindset.

★ Move at your pace. Avoid putting yourself in competition with other people because such unhealthy competition may lead you to develop some complexity that would make you feel like a failure.

SHARPEN YOUR SAW

Further reading

Here some recommended resources if you want to look at this topic in greater depth and expand your horizon on setting and achieving your goals.

Books:

- James Clear *Atomic Habits: An Easy & Proven Way to Build Good Habits & Break Bad Ones*

- John Lee Dumas *The 100-Day Goal Journal: Accomplish What Matters to You*

- Ruth Soukup, Abby Rike *Do it scared: finding the courage to face your fears, overcome adversity, and create a life you love*

- Tony Robbins *Awaken the Giant Within : How to Take Immediate Control of Your Mental, Emotional, Physical and Financial Destiny!*

DEVELOP THE RIGHT ATTITUDE FOR SUCCESS

"He who is not courageous enough to take risks will accomplish nothing in life."
Muhammad Ali

FAILURE IS A NECESSARY INGREDIENT TO ACHIEVE SUCCESS

Overcoming Your Fear of Failure

Fear is a fundamental part of human nature and the fear of not doing things correctly. And most times, it sabotages people's chances of becoming successful. Failing is definitely what nobody enjoys and the motivation to succeed is primarily triggered by the fear of failure. The fear of failure prevents people from trying, creates self-doubt, reduces self-confidence, and stalls progress, therefore, making one go against his or her morals, as well as reducing how much one can achieve in life.

There is no single reason why people develop a fear of failure. Rather, there are scores of reasons that constitute and contribute to the conscious and unconscious fear of failure in people.

We will examine what constitutes the fear of failure, how people acquire such fears, and how it can be overcome, in other to build confidence and enjoy optimum success in both our personal and professional life. Here are effective tips on how to overcome the fear of failure:

Learning from experience: One of the easiest ways of overcoming the fear of failure is learning from experience. There are times when things won't go as planned, and when it happens, that doesn't automatically mean that you have failed. It is paramount to have the mindset that there are lessons to be learned in every failure and to also note that every failure is an opportunity to grow and get things right. Learning that failure is a growth opportunity instead of a death sentence-- is the right step in the direction of overcoming failure and increasing your self-confidence. You need to start seeing failure as a blessing in disguise. Failure shouldn't stand in the way of your dreams. Since building confidence in one's ability can be learned, some of the strategies to build confidence will help pursue and achieve your goals.

Visualize the potential results: When setting your goals, or making important decisions, considering the potential result, both successes and failures, will make you naturally feel better at whatever outcome that you experience because you have had the chance to mentally anticipate what could happen. Therefore, anticipating the result of a task helps to reduce the uncertainty that can lead to anxiety and constant fear of failure. Forecasting the worst-case scenario is extremely helpful.

Have a backup plan: It is wise to always have a backup plan. People who have backup plans generally exude a high level of confidence in anything they want to do, which indirectly reduces their risk of failure. Having a backup plan enables you to take calculated risks, thereby opening to a wide range of solutions to tackling the problems, which will consequently reduce your fear of failure, and anxiety.

Be clear about your vision or purpose: Having a clarity of purpose or vision goes a long way in helping to reduce failure or fear of it. When taking on a task, it is very germane to have a specific purpose in mind and be clear about it. You also have to note, however, that there is always room for improvement and learning. The chances of failure will be reduced drastically if you aim for learning and improvement while accomplishing tasks.

Question yourself on the root cause of your negative beliefs: It is important to question yourself on the root cause of the negative beliefs that may have been your perspective about life. Ask yourself the way an outsider will do and try as much as possible to be very objective in your responses. It helps to pinpoint where you think the fears elicits from. The fear may come as far back as from your childhood, or long-existing insecurity.

Try to think positively: Our internal dialogue can play a huge role in affecting how we react and behave in situations. There is no gainsaying that we are a product of our thoughts and we believe what we tell ourselves. You must understand that even the most successful people encounter failure, for you to overcome the fear of failure. Try replacing your negative thoughts with positive ones about yourself. Remember that Steve Jobs was also once fired from Apple before he returned to be the face of the company for many years.

False self-confidence leads people to fear of failure: You need actual confidence. Not fake. Although, people who radiate true confidence are aware that they won't always succeed, thereby learning from their failure. However, for a perfectionist, failure can be so humiliating and terrible that they often don't want to try at all. The consequences of fear of failure can be so devastating on such individuals in their personal and professional life, which includes, loss of creativity, losing out on valuable opportunities, loss of valuable relationships, and regrets. To achieve your full potential, you need to overcome the fear of failure.

Patterns from childhood can cause people to have the fear of failure: Children who grow up on fear-based rules or in an atmosphere where there is frequently established ultimatum often end up assimilating such fears unconsciously. Excessive criticism of children by adults can cause the children to internalize a damaging mindset.

Overcoming the fear of failure doesn't happen by magic. For you to overcome this fear, you will have to project the worst-case scenario, and ask yourself these questions:

- What are the 3 possible positive things I can derive from the situation if at all I fail?

- What can I learn from the situation?

- How can I grow from the experience?

Having answered these questions, if at all you encounter failure in the quest of achieving your goals, you would have noted the benefits of the failure.

Actionable Advice

★ The fear of failure is what prevents you from trying or taking the necessary steps to achieve your goals.

★ The fear of failure will eat deep into your self-confidence and debar you from believing in yourself.

★ Ensure you learn from your mistakes, and other's people mistake to deal with your fear of failure.

★ You need to have a backup plan, as you will be able to take calculated risks.

★ Be optimistic. Replace your negative thoughts with positive ones.

"Remember: We all get what we tolerate. So, stop tolerating excuses within yourself, limiting beliefs of the past, or half-assed or fearful states."
Tony Robbins

SELF-LIMITING BELIEFS ARE BARRIERS BETWEEN YOU AND YOUR GOALS

Overcome Your Limiting Beliefs

Self-limiting beliefs are negative belief systems that we hold tightly which can hinder our growth. Our beliefs form the foundation of our expectation and purpose. Beliefs are crucial to the assumptions we make about ourselves, other people, and our expectations on how things ought to be in our world.

However, self-limiting beliefs are a particularly important factor, capable of ruining your confidence level as well as reduce your chances of achieving your goals. A lot of these self-limiting beliefs are acquired from childhood, and are difficult to jettison or outgrow, as they play an extremely negative role in reducing our chances of attaining success. Self-limiting beliefs drag one back from pushing and demanding what good things from life. More so, holding onto limiting beliefs is not a good decision because it can generally reduce your quality of relationship with others.

Here are steps that will help you overcome your limiting beliefs and help you take on life with fresh optimism and confidence:

Acknowledge that you possess certain limiting beliefs: Feigning ignorance to the problem won't help. The first step towards overcoming any problem is acknowledging that such a problem exists. If you don't admit the problem, it means that there is no problem to solve. Whereas the problem is right there in your front. Be honest with yourself. Pen down the limiting beliefs that are holding you down. Examine things that hold you down whenever you try to do something new. Don't be scared to add perfectionism to your limiting beliefs, if you feel like you cannot execute an idea unless it is perfect. You are one step close to overcoming them once you admit your limiting beliefs.

Identify and understand the reasons behind your limiting beliefs: This is also a very crucial aspect of overcoming your limiting beliefs. After identifying and understanding your limiting beliefs, examine them to find out different reasons that made you develop such beliefs. A lot of reasons are responsible for your self-limiting beliefs. It can be as a result of your childhood experiences or social interaction, or even your programming. For instance, some people find it hard to love again because of previous heartbreaks.

Face those reasons that are limiting your beliefs: You just have to face those limiting beliefs and understand that those beliefs could have been blown out of proportion. The fact that you have experienced heartbreak at some point does not rule out the possibilities that love exists in the universe. You need to realize that time will heal you. We will begin to see the rays of new possibilities and our confidence begins to build up when we begin to question these beliefs.

Understand the lies in these beliefs: Many of these beliefs we hold as true, are untrue, on a closer look. Why? Because in most cases, the foundation of these beliefs is very subjective. We believe most of these things as a psychological consequence of what has happened once to us, another person, or from what we have read. This will make the brain automatically shut down to the possibility of doing similar things because of what has been experienced or read. However, we can develop ourselves and increase our self-confidence by tweaking our mindset to believe a more positive one. We are one step closer to finally eschewing all forms of self-limiting beliefs, with this mindset.

Get new beliefs: To overcome self-limiting believes, you need to substitute the limiting beliefs with new and positive beliefs. You must make a conscious effort to switch from negative beliefs to a more inspiring new set of beliefs. However, in the process of selecting new beliefs, be careful in choosing those you can easily act on. It might take days, weeks, or months to assume new beliefs. It is impossible to assume that new personality overnight. However, with proper dedication and conscious acting, you will get there and build more confidence.

For example, if a previous terrible experience limits your belief that you cannot be a good tennis player, acquiring new beliefs by drawing inspiration from others success stories, taking up challenges to be better deliberately, and practicing being a good tennis player, will empower you to build your confidence and achieve your goals of being a professional tennis player.

Attempt this exercise to help you overcome your self-limiting beliefs:

Step 1: Pick a self-limiting belief you want to do away with. It can be, for example, a belief that you can't be happy in any relationship, or perhaps you want to stop limiting your finance.

Step 2: Note down a list of limiting beliefs you hold about the topic in question. Using money as an example, it can be something like:

- Money doesn't grow on trees
- Money is the root of all evil
- No one can be trusted with money
- The government is only interested in my money
- Taxes are my worst enemies
- I will always run out of money
- I can never have enough

Step 3: Be grateful to these beliefs for how they've "protected you." It is important that you honor these thoughts, even though it is counter-intuitive to thank them. It can't be denied that these beliefs have served a valid purpose. Using money as an example, the belief that you can't trust anyone with money might be birthed from your experience of being burnt by someone with money, and it is that belief that has protected you all these while from being burned once again.

Step 4: Don't be hard on yourself and forgive yourself for all the beliefs you have developed. You must be strong enough to forgive yourself for these beliefs. Forgive yourself for believing them, then forgive other people for causing you to have those beliefs.

Step 5: Allow yourself to acknowledge these beliefs and leave them in the past. Permit yourself to move past these self-limiting beliefs. Tap into the possibilities and concentrate on what is possible.

You should feel the emotions attached to these different beliefs changes, as you engage in these self-limiting beliefs. This will make you feel energetic and lighter.

This process can work for any part of your life you are experiencing a self-limiting belief.

Actionable Advice

★ Acknowledging that you have some self-limiting beliefs is the first step to overcoming your self-limiting beliefs.

★ Recognize the reasons why you develop these self-limiting beliefs.

★ Don't try to run away from those limiting beliefs. Face them squarely.

★ Understand the lies in these limiting beliefs.

★ Replace your self-limiting beliefs with healthy ones.

"We always hope for the easy fix: the one simple change that will erase a problem in a stroke. But few things in life work this way. Instead, success requires making a hundred small steps go right-- one after the other, no slipups, no goofs, everyone pitching in."
Atul Gawande

YOUR PROBLEMS ARE GUIDELINES TO SOMETHING GREATER

Having a Positive Attitude to Problem-solving

The art of making decisions and solving problems can be inculcated by anyone. Whenever a problem arises, some people make decisions effortlessly, but the reverse is the case for others, as taking a decision might constitute a big problem. These are the attitudes you must cultivate for you to be able to make effective decisions against your problems, and also help you achieve your goals.

1. Research attitude: When you can collect enough data, you will be able to see the problem from different angles. Collecting as much data as possible is the first step to solving any problem, before sitting to analyze the problem. By using the 5Ws: What? When? Where? Why? Who? You can adopt finding answers to your questions, for instance, when and where they have to do it? who will be doing what? You can go further to ask who will be affected by the decision? who must be consulted? Etc. This is one of the important attitudes you have to adopt.

2. The attitude of taking your time: You need to create time to concentrate on the problem if you want to solve a problem. You will end up becoming distracted or confused if you attempt to find a solution while engaged in other activities.

Whenever you wake up, don't just jump out of the bed. Give yourself some time, 17 minutes is enough to ponder on your problem. That moment, before being fully awake, you will find out the time is largely productive for clear thinking. You need to know when your brain functions better for you to be able to create the appropriate time. Note that the time you select also matters because there are times when our brain functions better. But generally, the best time is when you are just waking, because your mind will still be at work with the same wavelength that produced your dreams.

The end of the day is their best time to think clearly, for some people, which is after finishing the day's work or other activities. This is when their brain switches to a creative mode. Their level of tiredness will be what will decide if they will be productive or not. But the best way to stay productive for these people to practice relaxation techniques for the day, and engage in meditation, or, before focusing on their problems.

If you are in this category, you can experiment with going to bed 15 minutes earlier than usual. Get a journal and focus on your problems when you are in this state. While some can only focus on their problems, when about to sleep. The creative mind takes over when they are feeling drowsy. Although this doesn't necessarily keep you awake, but it will clear your mind. You can set aside time to do this if that time is not convenient for you.

Therefore, try as much as possible to inculcate the attitude of setting aside time to look into your problem.

3. Brainstorming attitude: You need the attitude of brainstorming whenever you want to solve problems. There are two ways in which this can be done. True brain-storm style is the first way. This needs to be done in a group because ideas grow when you are deliberating on an already established idea. That is, you can invite trusted friends or families (experienced) to give you their honest opinion or idea. You will want people to generate ideas for you, not defend, therefore don't criticize any ideas. The quality of an idea does not matter in this situation, it is the quantity. Also, if your problem is confidential, you can do your brainstorming in writing. Whatever occurs to you should be noted You can then go ahead to sort out which ideas are feasible, and which ones are not.

4. A attitude that redefines problems: The solution to a problem solely relies on how it is stated. You will get a limited and narrow answer if you define it narrowly. A whole range of possibilities is opened if you can redefine your problems. That said, a question like "How will I buy new Christmas clothes? Will become something like: "How can I look exceptional on Christmas day?

5. A attitude of optimism: We only ensure failure in life by assuming the worst will happen, or by just accepting what happens. It is common for a lot of people to already give in even before a problem began. For instance, you may believe that you will never buy a car, and the thought will show in your attitude, making you not making the effort to save to buy a car.

6. Never die attitude: Only by continuous trial, you will increase your chances of getting things done. This should be your approach to life. Continue trying, if at first, you don't succeed, although, this might seem corny, that is the truth. The attitude of not giving up is not only helpful in your problem solving, but it is also applicable in every part of our existence.

Here are tips that can aid you in solving your problems:

- Reflect on your response to problems.

- Define the problem by asking yourself some key questions.

- Establish creativity in your option for solving a problem.

- Find the root cause and avoid solving the symptoms.

- Use the potential and power of tea, to solve problems.

Actionable Advice

★ You need to be optimistic to be able to solve problems.

★ You must develop a never die attitude towards problem-solving. That is, the attitude of always going back to solve the problem.

★ The attitude of redefining a problem, or considering other perspectives is helpful in solving a problem.

★ A brainstorming attitude is also especially important in solving problems.

★ You need to acquire the attitude of research.

"He who every morning plans the transactions of that day and follows that plan carriers a thread that will guide him through the labyrinth of the busiest life."
Victor Hugo

NEVER TAKE YOUR TIME FOR GRANTED

Regaining Control Over Your Time

The first thing you should learn and know is how to define time management. A lot of people don't know and understand what it truly is. Time management could be defined as *"one's ability to use one's time productively or effectively, especially at work."* Just as Jim Rohn once said, *"Either run the day or the day runs you."* Ways to avoid being run by your day and improve your time management skills will be discussed here if you feel as though you are always being run by your day.

Businesses in the world work around Benjamin Franklin's quote "time is money". This means that the more time you make, the more money you make. And, over the years different professionals have continuously developed the idea and practice of time management. And this is mainly due to the idea of time management as an actual concept that came about in the 19th century with the Industrial

Revolution. It wasn't that people weren't able to manage their time before that period, but that was when the change began. The increase in factory works created a new type of workplace and made it necessary for people to begin to manage their time differently.

What is time management?

When it comes down to knowing how to define time management people are confused. Though they understand that there are different ways to get more accomplished. Time management is something people talk about a lot, nowadays. They seem to struggle more with getting things done even though we all have the same 24 hours that people had hundreds of years ago. But there is this sense of busyness that we carry through the day with us.

However, time management all boils down to the way each person uses their time each day. Some people seem to have a natural gift for knowing how to do this, but the truth is, it's something that everyone can easily do. A lot of people believe that there is a trick to time management. They believe that some people seem to have a secret to being able to get more done in a shorter period.

High achievers seem to get so much done when other people seem to accomplish nothing in a day given the same amount of time. You can either decide to control your day or allow your day to control you and controlling your day can be achievable by managing the time given to you. So, time management is the way you choose to spend your time.

What is poor time management?

It is often running late for your day. Running out the door or leaving home for where you are going at the last minute, sleeping too late, showing up for a meeting at the nick of time. Procrastination and barely meeting deadlines is poor management of time too. A lot of people know what poor management of time looks and feels like.

You could go out the door smoothly and be on time with a good attitude if you manage your time better before needing to leave wherever you are. But when you aren't able to go out smoothly, there is a tendency that you will fight with your family, friends, colleagues, or co-workers as you try to get out the door. Because when you constantly feel like you have to rush and don't have enough time, it's easier to lose your temper with those around you. Therefore, when you have poor time management skills, it impacts every area of your life.

What is good time management?

When you manage your time very well in a day, you are more productive and a more efficient worker. You work smarter instead of harder. You stress yourself less and accomplish most things you need to do at ease when you manage your time efficiently. Good time management opens new doors for you as you become more organized and produce higher-quality work. It also allows you to rise above the level that you were previously when you manage it properly.

Time management includes what?

Certain skills are required to have good time management abilities. These skills can be broken down into making decisions, setting goals, prioritizing, and planning, task delegation, and scheduling.

The fact is that there isn't one way that needs to be improved to manage your time. A lot of things are involved in the process of time management. Therefore, you will need to focus on different ways to boost your time management skills if you are looking for a means to increase your productivity.

Goal setting

The first step you should consider focusing on time management should be the setting of goals. Because it will help to lead you throughout the rest of the process. There isn't a purpose for your time management skills to be improved if you have no goal. If you have no goal in mind, it doesn't matter whether you define time management, nothing will change. Setting goals is a pivotal part of time management because it gives you an overall focus on what you wish to accomplish.

Making decisions

You could end up wasting much of your time in a day if you struggle with making decisions. Because when it comes to time management, decision-making skill is a pivotal tool to have.

For the things that truly matter, high achievers know that they need to save their ability to make decisions. And that's why, for example, Mark Zuckerberg wears the same grey T-shirt each day because it eliminates the need to decide what he needs to wear. Highest achievers work fervently to lessen the number of decisions they are expected to make each day.

Prioritizing and planning

Planning makes you see and understand when you don't have enough time to complete a task that needs to be done. It also permits you to discover if a task you'll like to accomplish will fit into your daily activities. But the first thing should be your priorities. You need to prioritize. And this means you'll first establish the things you need to give more attention to or the most important things. You can start making your plans immediately you know or set your priorities. Both priorities and plans go hand-in-hand when you are working to define time management.

DEVELOP THE RIGHT ATTITUDE FOR SUCCESS

When you stick with creating and following a plan daily, you'll find out that you are getting things done easily and you are more productive. However, if you are not the type who usually plans your day, this may be difficult to get used to.

Task delegation

At times, you may discover that there are many things you ought to accomplish in a single day, whereas there is a limit to what only you can accomplish. However, you can consider delegating tasks to others to get a lot more accomplished. When delegating tasks to people, it's also important you consider the type of tasks that are being handed off to someone else. By considering delegating a task, you should choose someone great or suitable for the job and then trust them with the task. A lot of people struggle with a delegation of tasks because as they turn the task to someone else, they still partake in it. And that may frustrate the person which the work was given to. It's likely to eat up your valuable time too.

Scheduling

You won't do more than what you can do when you schedule and put into account every task on your to-do list. You ought to know what to do at a time and have a realistic plan for your schedule. Because the better control you have over your time, the better control you have over your schedules. However, no matter how many types of instruments or tools you have in place, if you have too much on your to-do list, you won't be able to accomplish as many tasks as you intend.

Time management consists of different skills as you can see. Many people struggle with it despite that it looks or sounds as though it's something very simple. And different people struggle with time management for different reasons.

Without managing your time well, you will become stressed and overwhelmed when you constantly feel like you're running behind, missing deadlines, and taking on more than you can handle. And that can both mentally and physically take a toll on you. So, time management doesn't only increase your level of happiness but also often affects your productivity.

DEVELOP THE RIGHT ATTITUDE FOR SUCCESS

> **Actionable Advice**
>
> ★ Regaining control over your time requires you to be able to identify tasks you can do yourself, and the ones you can delegate to others.
>
> ★ You need to take prioritization and planning seriously to regain control over your time.
>
> ★ Have a goal in mind you wish to achieve at the end of the day.
>
> ★ Reduce the number of decisions you have to make, by only focusing on things that matter.
>
> ★ Have a realistic plan for your Schedule.

"A year from now, you may wish you had started today."
Karen Lamb

DO WHATEVER YOU CAN DO, RIGHT THIS MOMENT!

Dealing with Procrastination

Laziness and procrastination are two different things. But people often confuse procrastination with being lazy. Laziness suggests apathy, an unwillingness to act, and inactivity. In contrast, procrastination is choosing to do something else instead of the task you are supposed to be doing. It most times involves avoiding a task you don't like, but the task is likely to be very important, in favor of a task that is easier or enjoyable.

Procrastination can result in missing out on achieving your goals and can lead to a reduction in productivity. For instance, slight occurrences of procrastination can make you feel bad or ashamed. And this impulse can give birth to significant consequences.

In extreme cases, you can be demotivated and disillusioned with your work, which can lead to depression and even job loss if you procrastinate over a long period.

When people see a task unpleasantly, they are more likely to put it off. More recent research suggests procrastination is linked to difficulty managing distress while that may be true for some. In psychology, it has long been believed that people who procrastinate have a faulty sense of time— that they think they'll have more time to get something done than they do.

What's more, procrastination can hinder self-critical thoughts that can result from putting off tasks, your self-esteem with guilt or shame. Procrastinators tend to have more sleep issues and experience greater stressful regret than non-procrastinators.

Procrastination can also lead to increased stress, health problems, and poorer performance. This approach can ironically cause more distress in the long run while procrastinators may be trying to avoid distress.

It is possible to overcome procrastination as with most bad habits. Try any of these tips, which will be listed below, to get you on track if you struggle with putting things off.

Recognizing procrastination

You probably are procrastinating if you start putting things off indefinitely, or switch focus because you want to avoid doing something. However, you aren't necessarily procrastinating if you're briefly delaying an important task for a genuinely good reason. You might be putting off a task because you've had to re-prioritize your workload.

These are other ways to know if you are procrastinating too:

- You'll be procrastinating if your day is filled with tasks with low priority.

- You may also be procrastinating by leaving a pivotal item on your to-do list for a long time.

- You'll most likely procrastinate when you take or fill your to-do list with trivial tasks that other people ask you to do instead of getting on with the pivotal tasks you already have.

- You may likely procrastinate if you've started a high-priority task and later go off to make a coffee.

- Waiting for the right time or wanting to be in the right mood to tackle a task can lead to procrastination.

- Reading emails over and over without making any decision on what to do with them can also lead to procrastination.

Why you procrastinate

Before you could begin tackling procrastination, you need to understand why you procrastinate.

For example, if you avoid a task because you find it uninteresting or unpleasant, you can quickly take some steps to get that unpleasant task out of your way so that you can focus on the aspects of your job that you find more enjoyable.

Not being well organized could lead to procrastination. People who are organized successfully overcome procrastination because they create effective schedules and use prioritized to-do lists. To organize your tasks by priority and deadline, there a lot of things that would help you.

You can be organized and still feel overwhelmed by a task. Possibly you worry too much about failing and doubt your ability to carry out a task. So, you seek comfort in what you're capable of completing and put the task off.

Some usually think success will lead them to be swamped with the request to take on more tasks. And success is being feared by them as much as failure.

Rather than doing something imperfectly, perfectionists would rather avoid doing a task they don't feel they have enough skills or experience to do. Surprisingly, perfectionists are usually procrastinators.

You'll most likely put off taking action in case you do the wrong thing if you can't decide what to do. And poor decision-making is another major cause of procrastination.

Adopting of Anti-procrastination Strategies

To give yourself the best chance of succeeding, try as much as possible to adopt different strategies that will be provided below. Because habits only stop being habits when you avoid practicing them. And procrastination is a deeply ingrained pattern of behavior that you probably can't break overnight.

To reduce the likelihood of procrastination in the future, studies have shown that self-forgiveness can help you to feel more positive about yourself. You should forgive yourself for procrastinating in the past.

Write down and specify a time you need to complete tasks. Stay committed to the tasks, focus on doing and accomplishing, but not avoid. To proactively tackle your work, this will help you.

Make sure you notice how good it feels to finish things. Reward yourself with a treat, such as a coffee from your favorite coffee shop or a slice of cake if you complete a difficult task at the stipulated time. So, make sure you promise yourself a reward at the beginning of the task.

You can also ask someone to check up on you because peer pressure works, and this is a principle behind self-help groups. But if you don't have anyone to ask in checking up on you, you can use an online tool such as Procraster to help to monitor yourself.

Rather than allowing your tasks to build up over another day, make sure you act as you go and tackle them as soon as they arise.

While you work be sure that you switched off the notification of your social media handles and email and avoid sitting anywhere close to the television to minimize distraction.

The first thing your aim should be every day is to *"eat an elephant beetle"*. Be certain that you get the tasks you find least pleasant out of your way as early as possible, in a day. Doing that will give you the rest of the day to concentrate on work that you find more enjoyable.

You will feel more in control of your workload when you adopt the usage of the phrase "I choose to," which implies that you own a project. However, it could make you feel disempowered and might even result in self-sabotage. But when you rephrase your internal dialog and adopt the phrase "I need to" and "I have to," for example, it implies you have no other choice rather than to do it.

Combat procrastination by identifying the long-term benefits of completing a task. For example, ask yourself if it could affect your end-of-year bonus or annual performance review. Research has also shown that people who are impulsive and focused on short-term gain or benefits are more likely to procrastinate. Try to focus on the *"long game"* if you procrastinate because you find a task unpleasant.

One other way to make a task more enjoyable is to identify the unpleasant consequences of avoiding or ignoring it and how it might affect your personal, team, or organizational goals. For example, ask yourself what will happen if you don't complete the work.

At the same time, you need to give a task a try at times. Because you may find it not as bad as you thought. So, it's important to acknowledge that we can often overestimate the unpleasantness of a task. But it can be useful to reframe the task by looking at its meaning and relevance. And this will increase its value to you and make your work more worthwhile.

Here are some strategies to help you get organized if you procrastinate:

- Keeping a to-do list will prevent you from "conveniently" forgetting about those overwhelming or unpleasant tasks.

- Prioritizing your to-do list by using Eisenhower's Urgent/Important Principle will enable you to quickly identify the activities you should ignore and those you should focus on as well.

- Turn yourself into a master of scheduling and project planning. If you don't know where to start when you have multiple or a big project at once, tools like this can help you reduce your stress levels and plan your time effectively.

- Do the tasks that you find most difficult at these times and identify when you're most effective. Know the time you work better, know whether you work best in the morning, the afternoon, or at night. Just make sure you tackle the hardest tasks at your peak times.

- Give yourself a specific deadline to accomplish tasks will keep you on track to achieve your goals which will also mean that you have no time for procrastination. So, set yourself time-bound goals.

- A lot of apps have been designed to help you to be more organized. You can use task- and time-management apps to achieve and accomplish a lot of tasks.

- Organize your projects into smaller tasks and focus on starting them, rather than finishing them. Try to break them down into more manageable chunks if you're prone to delaying projects because you find them overwhelming or unpleasant.

Small wins will make you feel more positive and less overwhelmed by the larger project or goal that you are working towards, and that will give you a sense of achievement. It's good to start with quick and small tasks first. Jeffery Combs in his 2011 book, "The Procrastination Cure," suggests that tackling tasks in 15-minute bursts of activity. Substitutionally, you can create an action plan to organize your project.

In conclusion, take a look at this range of decision-making tips to help you to develop yours if you think you put something off because you can't decide what action to take or you find it hard to make decisions.

Actionable Advice

★ Get used to using "I have to" and "I need to" when noting your tasks.

★ Deal with procrastination by identifying the long-term benefit of completing the task now.

★ Make your tasks enjoyable.

★ Categorize your tasks into what you must do now, and what can wait.

★ Always have a specific deadline for each of your tasks.

Further reading

Here some recommended resources if you want to look at this topic in greater depth and expand your horizon on setting and achieving your goals.

Books:

- Idil Ahmed. *Manifest Now*

- Brian Tracy and Berrett-Koehler Publishers. *Eat That Frog!: 21 Great Ways to Stop Procrastinating and Get More Done in Less*

- John C. Maxwell. *How Successful People Think: Change Your Thinking, Change Your Life*

- S.J. Scott. *How to Stop Procrastinating: A Simple Guide to Mastering Difficult Tasks and Breaking the Procrastination Habit*

- Damon Zahariades. *The Procrastination Cure: 21 Proven Tactics For Conquering Your Inner Procrastinator, Mastering Your Time, And Boosting Your Productivity!*

- Frank Bettger. *How I Raised Myself from Failure to Success in Selling*

LET'S ACHIEVE YOUR GOALS

"Eat a live frog first thing in the morning and nothing worse will happen to you the rest of the day."
Mark Twain

DO THE MOST IMPORTANT THINGS FIRST!

The 80/20 Rule

One of the most renowned concepts of management and life goal is the 80/20 principle. Also known as the Pareto principle, this principle states that 80 percent of our comes from the most important 20 percent of what we do.

In 1895, this principle was named after Vilfredo Pareto, the Italian economist. Vilfredo stated that people naturally divide into what he tagged the top 20 percent or "vital few" about influence or money, and the "trivial many", or the bottom 80 percent.

As at the time Vilfredo established this principle, he found out that 80 percent of the wealth in Italy was in the hands, and controlled by, just 20 percent of the Italian population. It was later he discovered that this principle applies to almost every economic activity.

The 80/20 principle can be applied to any situation you could imagine. Hence, having a good grasp of this principle can teach you the importance of prioritizing your tasks, according to the days, weeks, and months.

The world's major business and political leaders understand that this principle is very essential to strategic planning. However, this part of the book will focus on how this principle can be applied in setting your goals and becoming more productive.

The Idea Behind Pareto Principle

The central meaning of this principle establishes that on a to-do list, 2 of 10 items, are more or greater worth than the other 8 items put together.

According to this principle, the top ten or twenty percent of items that are unbelievably valuable and important are what a lot of people procrastinate. This is known as the "vital few". As aforementioned, while on the other hand, the other 80 percent which is the least important, contributes little or nothing to our success, and this we know to be the "trivial many."

Use the following table to prioritize your tasks:

Impact towards you goals	Effort / time required	What to do? How to face/approach these tasks?
High	Low	Do this first! These actions will have the biggest return on invest from your time/effort.
High	High	Can this task be split into smaller tasks? If so, do it and use the same technique with the smaller tasks. Alternatively, if this is not possible consider delegating. Especially if you are not great with this specific task or do not possess the required skill or expertise, thus, increasing the effort it requires from you.
Low	Low	Consider delegating this task or doing it during valley periods. Since the time/effort required is low, you might be able to do them even when your energy or motivation is low.
Low	High	Discard these tasks! Ask yourself why it is compulsory to do this. In most cases it is not necessary to do this type of tasks and they can be easily discarded with minor or no impact at all. Actually, overall impact might be positive, since by not doing these actions, you might have more energy and time to devote to the real impactful ones,

Using this rule to goal setting

These are what you should do to apply the 80/20 rule, for you to set smart goals that will boost your productivity:

Write down 10 goals you wish to achieve on a piece of paper, ask yourself this question, after writing down the goals: "If I could achieve it today, which of these goals will make the biggest impact in my life?"

Afterward, write down your second most important goal. You would discover that you have determined the most important 20 percent of your goal that will help you more than anything else, by the time you are done with the exercise. The most valuable goals, that is, the 20 percent you choose should be given more attention and time.

First, eat the biggest frog

Have you noticed how some people are always terribly busy, but they seem to have only achieved little or sometimes nothing, at the end of the day? The reason is that people in this category waste their time working on things that will bring them little or no reward while postponing or procrastinate on the 20 percent that could offer a big difference in their personal, and professional life.

The question you should always ask yourself before you begin any work is: "Does this task I am about to engage in part of my top 20 or the 80 percent?" The most important and valuable tasks you can engage yourself in every day are the most complex, and hardest tasks, which will have a tremendous impact on your long pursuit.

Starting your daily activities with tasks that have low value in your list of goals will make you eventually develop the habit of always starting and working on a low-value task.

The most important rule of this principle is resisting the urge to clear up small things first.

Achieving Success in Life with the Pareto Rule

It has always been the way that great success and achievement have the same starting point. The starting point of both begins with dreaming big.

It will be exceedingly difficult to attain that success if you don't cast off your limitations and begin to fantasize about what you will experience. Your level of self-esteem and confidence will grow when you start dreaming big. Most people don't achieve success because they have never sat down to imagine the kind of life they could live. It was once said that only big dreams can move the mind of men, and we must be bold enough to dream big. Dreaming big will equip you with the power to handle whatever happens to you.

The Theory of Constraint

The discovery of Goldratt made us understand that every process that will lead to a goal, has a choke, or a bottleneck that prevent that goal from being actualized. This theory is one of the breakthroughs in modern thinking. Elihu Goldratt propounded the theory of constraints, and it is a powerful theory that allows you to dream without boundaries. This theory also clarifies that the speed at which this goal is actualized is determined by this constraint.

Goldratt's discovery states that diverting all your creative energies, and attention on pushing off your identified constraint can expedite the process rather than doing any other single thing.

For instance, if you would like to increase your income, but you know that there are constraints holding you from achieving that goal. If you can't pinpoint the constraints, you may want to ask yourself this question: "What is the constraint preventing or holding me back, or deciding the speed at which I increase my income?"

As you know, your income is a reward for the quality and quantity of the work you do at your place of work. So, all you may have to do is just to increase the quantity and quality of the job to increase that income. Another option can be to change your job to the one that pays twice as the one you are currently doing.

Identifying Your Productivity Constraint

What is your constraint? What is deciding the speed at which you achieve your goal? Your skill or your level of education? Is it the situation that you are in today? Is it your level of health or environment? Is it your occupation or job?

Most people find it difficult to identify the things standing between them, and their goals. What they do most times is to create excuses and feel helpless. You can probably get yourself out in whatever situation you have gotten yourself into. Understand that you can unlearn whatever you have learned. You can set this as your standard and compare everything that you do against it if your real goal is to dream big and live without limits.

Actionable Advice

★ On your to-do list, 2 of 10 items, are more or greater worth than the other 8 items put together.

★ Starting your daily activities with tasks that have low value in your list of goals will make you eventually develop the habit of always starting and working on a low-value task.

★ Most people don't achieve success because they have never sat down to imagine the kind of life they could live.

★ The speed at which this goal is actualized is determined by this constraint.

★ Understand that you can unlearn whatever you have learned.

"The goal you set must be challenging. At the same time, it should be realistic and attainable, not impossible to reach. It should be challenging enough to make you stretch, but not so far that you break."
Rick Hansen

YOU MUST SET REALISTIC GOALS IN ORDER TO ACHIEVE THEM

Effective Steps to Setting and Achieving Realistic Goals

You will lack direction and focus without setting your goals. You are put in the driver's seat of your life when you set goals. This is what gives you the power to change your life in the direction you deem fit. In many circumstances, the goals we set out to complete are abandoned and left incomplete somewhere along the line.

You need to know how to set your goals, for you to be able to accomplish them. And it starts with careful consideration, then hard work, for you to make the best use of the process, and for you to be able to achieve what you set out to achieve. These are helpful steps, in setting effective goals.

1. Trust the Process

Trusting and having absolute faith in the process is the first approach to setting effective goals. You might as well forget your attempt to achieve your goals if you don't have the confidence in yourself and your ability. Turn your thought into reality. Everything you can see begins as a goal in someone's head.

2. Write it down

You have to plan for an attack, in order for you to eventuate the goal. It is important that you write down your goals and attach a timeline to achieving them. Writing down your goals is the key to success, as it will put you back on track if you derail from the path to your goal. Neglecting this step will make you forget your goals or reduce their importance. When you have your goals written somewhere, it will increase their value and significance, thereby, inspiring you to achieve them.

3. Set specific goals

If your goals deal with specific facts and events, it has a much greater chance of being accomplished. Your goals can easily be skipped over or misconstrued if your direction is vague. Specific goals give regimen and precision to your objectives.

4. Set measurable goals

You will be able to work towards the achievement of your goals if they are able to adhere to concrete criteria. You will know that you have accomplished something tangible if you can identify what you see, hear, and feel when you reach your goals. You should break your goals down into measurable elements, in order to achieve effective goal setting.

5. Set attainable goals

It is crucial for you to measure if the goal applies to your lifestyle. Although, there is nothing wrong with shooting for the stars. You will be setting yourself up to fail and most certainly be miserable if you don't have money, experience, and time to achieve something. Ensure you are planning your steps wisely and establishing a realistic time frame that will allow you to carry out these steps for the most effective goal setting.

6. Set realistic goals

To be realistic, your goals have to represent an objective which you are willing and able to work towards. Nothing demotivates more than not being able to achieve something you set up to do. You are the only one that can determine how substantial your goal should be. However, you have to give space for realistic chances that give the appropriate circumstances, you will be able to achieve your goals.

7. Set timely goals

There is no sense of urgency without a time frame. Every set goal must be grounded within a time frame. It is important that you attach a time frame in which you want to achieve it. If you have deadlines for your goals, it will help you work towards them, and create motivation that will keep your high morale. However, it can be extremely sensitive and tricky setting a time frame for your goals, but you can be motivated by being stringent with the timely aspect of it. The other side of this is that you can become demotivated if you are not ticking the box on your scheduled dates.

8. Stay accountable

Things are bound to get tough when you are working towards a goal. You must hold yourself accountable when facing adversity.

Telling your friends and family may give you the responsibility you need, and helping you build a support system that will give you the strength to continue to push further. You have to surround yourself with constant encouragement from those who are following your progress if you want to remain accountable in your daily life.

9. Don't be scared of asking

It is essential to learn from those around you when entering a new venture. There is nothing to be ashamed of in asking for help, because gathering experience from others may be the only thing that sets you apart. Seeking advice can come in different forms, it can be developing a mentor, asking a friend, or from a variety of people. It has been discovered that going back to study is one of the most helpful ways when attempting to achieve a goal.

10. Assess your progress periodically

Our goals are constantly evolving and changing, as time goes on. Although, the outcome may not be what we have in our mind, but it can sometimes be a good thing. Constantly assessing your progress throughout your goal-setting journey will give you the opportunity to learn from your mistakes and assist you in setting your goals next time.

Here some likely tools you will need to keep in track, and stay focused on achieving your goals:

- A journal or a handwritten diary to track your smaller achievements and goals
- Your phone can also be helpful in setting daily countdown app, or reminder for when you need to achieve certain things

- Have a friendly reminder in form of motivational notes, and posters on your work desk, or around your home

- Telling family and friends what you are working towards so that they can support you

- Mindfulness, positive affirmation, and meditation are some of the visualization activities you should practice.

Also, to effectively set realistic goals, you can practice this exercise:

This exercise can be done on a computer, notebook, or your journal. The exercise is known as the "Average Perfect Day" exercise. It is very straightforward, just like the name suggests. All you have to do is just to note down, step-by-step, how your average day looks like.

Without any added surprise or extras, focus on what your perfect day looks like. What you are doing here is to create a detailed list of how your average day looks like. It could be something like:

- Starting from the time you mostly wake in the morning, what does it look like? Do you do a sun salutation or mindfulness to start your day? Do you read for 20 minutes before getting up, or you cuddle with your partner?

- Once you are out of bed, what do you do? Do you shower first, or bake snacks for breakfast? Is the window blind, or curtain opened fully, or you like them closed as you get ready? Is there radio, TV, or music in the background? Do you pick out your outfit for the day, or you've done that a night before?

- What is the next thing? Do go to work? How does it feel working? Who are the people you engage with? Can you describe what your table looks like?

- Are you back home to your family? What do you do when you are home? What adventures or activities do you do together?

- What does your nutrition lunch include or look like?

List each of your activities and be detailed. Do this for 5 to 7 days a week, preferably a day you will never get bored of. For your downtime and workdays, create an "Average Perfect Day."

Do this without or with your kids and partner. Reflect on the individual behavior that goes into the day. It will become visible to you that there are some habits that you can start right away that will push you towards your idea of a perfect average day.

Actionable Advice

★ Without setting your goals, you will lack direction and focus.

★ For you to be able to accomplish your goals, you need to know how to set them.

★ The first approach to setting effective goals is trusting and having absolute faith in the process.

★ Don't forget to write down your goals.

★ There is no sense of urgency without a time frame. Every set goal must be grounded within a time frame.

Further reading

Here some recommended resources if you want to look at this topic in greater depth and expand your horizon on setting and achieving your goals.

Books:

- David Goggins. *Can't Hurt Me: Master Your Mind and Defy the Odds*

- Joseph Murphy. *The Power of Your Subconscious Mind*

- Gary Keller and Jay Papasan. *The ONE Thing: The Surprisingly Simple Truth Behind Extraordinary Results*

- Simon Sinek. *Start with Why: How Great Leaders Inspire Everyone to Take Action*

THE PATH TO ACHIEVING YOUR GOALS

"When one can accept that all their circumstances and life events are a result of their decision making, that individual immediately gain back their power to create."
Michael Austin Jacobs

EVERYTHING START WITH A DECISION

Important Tips to Making Your Most Important Decisions

It can take a great deal of practice for you to feel confident and comfortable in your choices. It is not easy to make decisions. These are important tips for making effective decisions:

1. **Create some quiet time**

You don't have to surround yourself with distractions, such as nonstop email, ringing phones, the constant buzz of chatter from those around you, etc. if you are about to make an important decision.

Decide on a place or time, where you will be undisturbed when about to begin the process of decision making. It doesn't have to be a long time, as far as it is effective. If you feel you will need more time, you can set aside some more time on another date, and make it a decision-making time. Just make sure you are in a quiet place, and that no one is disturbing you from concentrating.

It is equally crucial not to make a major decision when you are hungry and tired or don't feel well, or perhaps emotionally unstable, or physically worn out, or when you are under an undue deal of pleasure.

2. **Clear your head**

There are times when there will be a lot happening or going on in your head, with most of it not having anything to do with the decision you are about to make. A calm and centered mind is the best foundation for effective decision-making. Deep breathing, as well as yoga and prayer, can help, or whatever you feel will help you clear the chatters in your head. Do some meditation to clear the noise in your head.

3. **Be clear about your goals**

Take some time to think about what you really want, what you are ready to work for, and the result you want to achieve. Most times, different goals are swirling in your head. This might confuse you and make you want to give up the decision-making process because you are not sure which one should rise top. Such goal clarity is important to arrive at a workable, sound decision.

4. **Have a timetable for yourself**

The bigger the decision, the higher the likelihood of it slipping off without a concrete timetable to adhere to. Decisions must have a timetable. Otherwise, actions will be put off and delayed in favor of other distractions and activities. For you to gauge if you are faring and adjusting accordingly, try giving yourself a progress check often.

5. Gather information

Any important decision requires that you have a certain amount of information to conclude from. There are some decisions you can't make without researching, gathering information, and confirming sources, as applicable. Hence, gathering a considerable amount of information is part of your decision-making process on important issues.

6. Identify your bias

We all have biases, so it is nothing unusual. You are sometimes oblivious that you hold a certain degree of bias in some areas. It will reflect on your choices, making your decision as effective as you would want it to if you however fail to recognize your biases. If you need help in that area, you can ask a trusted friend what they see to be your biases.

7. Always try to be objective

In addition to watching out for your bias, always try to strive for objectivity in your decision-making process. It is important to be very objective when it comes to making a decision, because your decisions may be life-altering. Objectivity is like a neutral ground, an interim step you settle on before you continue to make further choices.

8. Pay attention to your instinct

Consider listening to what your instinct tells you, as they are often right when it comes to what is best for you, or what you should note before making any decision. Some people call it relying on the gut, while some other people call it the sixth sense.

9. Table the facts

Avoid skipping this step because it will distort your decision. You need to be able to gather the facts before moving on. For you to be able to view it more objectively, write down everything you know about the decision you are about to take on a paper.

10. Consider both the pros and cons

You are moving closer to the point where you will be able to decide, so make sure you weigh the pros and cons. There is always a plus or minus to consider, in every decision. While some can be obvious, others can only be through careful analysis of the fact, or knowledge acquired from experience, or advice from experts, friends, family, or coworkers.

11. Envision the consequence of your action

If what you are envisioning is desirable, then that should help you solidify your choice. Is the risk you are putting worth the ultimate good? Are you willing to go ahead if it's negative? Imagine what will happen if you decide on an action. Try to envision the consequences in your mind.

12. Think of how your decision will square with your values

Any of the decisions you make should fit your values. Always be sincere with your values, since they are the core of the person you are. There are times when you will be pressured to make a decision that doesn't feel right probably by your boss, family member, coworker, or friends. The decision doesn't feel right because it doesn't align with your values. You will be dissatisfied if you eventually fall in line with what you are asked to do.

13. Factor in follow-up

It is also important you take time to follow up with the choices you have made. Did they pan out as anticipated? Were you able to arrive at your objectives and arrive at your goal? Note that whatever decision you make doesn't make it the end of your decision-making process. If you are making such a decision again, is there a way you can improve upon it? Can you revise your current actions to make your choice better?

14. Make an informed choice

After going through all these listed steps, you are ready to finally make an informed decision. This is what the decision-making process entails, and you have conducted yourself thoroughly and thoughtfully. Proceed with certainty and choose what you are going to do. Make your decision.

15. Act on your decision

You must act on your decision after going for it. Note that thoughts without actions to back them up are ineffective. It is now time to act on it. As Pablo Picasso once said, *"Action is the foundational element of success."* You have invested a considerable amount of your time to get this far, and you have put a lot of diligence to arrive at making a decision.

Actionable Advice

★ Create a space for yourself to think.

★ Ensure that you are in the right frame of mind before taking any decision.

★ Gather enough information as possible to support your decisions.

★ Recognize your bias when taking a decision.

★ Pay attention to your instinct.

"Change is the law of life. And those we look only to the past or present are certain to miss the future."
John F Kennedy

YOU HAVE TO BE FLEXIBLE TO NAVIGATE LIFE SUCCESSFULLY

Adapting to Change

Change is unavoidable, and it gets tougher the more we resist it. According to how Kennedy quoted it, change is a law life. Change is one of the most dramatic impacts on our lives, as we are surrounded by it. You don't have to avoid it. It will find you, force you to reconsider, and challenge you on how to live life.

Why must you adapt to change?

It can be as a result of crisis, choice, or by just chance, change will come into our life. The choice is always in front of us-- do we make the change or not?

It is better to be prepared for change because our reaction to it will be in our circle of control. You will lose control of your reaction to change if you are unprepared or resistant to it. This means that you will be living your life as a reactionary, instead of an activator.

"Life is a series of natural and spontaneous changes. Don't resist them; that only creates sorrow. Let reality be the reality. Let things flow naturally forward in whatever way they like." -- Lao Tzu

There is no way we can prepare for unexpected events. They will always happen, and these events are what shift us away from our comfort zone, thereby forcing us to change. We will be denying ourselves the opportunity to learn and grow if we ignore or hide away from the challenge of change.

"To exist is to change, to change is to mature, to mature is to go on creating oneself endlessly." -- Henri Bergson

When we embrace change in a positive way, our resilience in life can grow stronger, rather than ignore, and hide from the opportunity that change can bring to our lives.

You can't escape the impact change will bring to your life. Do you want to live a life where you know you are thriving? Then you must embrace change.

Ways to Adapt to Change

1. The power of choice – Change your mindset

"Progress is impossible without change, and those who cannot change their mindset cannot change anything" -- George Bernard Shaw

We all love the comfort zone. The reason our subconscious likes it is because, it is the known, as embracing change means stepping into the unknown, which our subconscious is not in support of. Therefore, it resists.

When we are faced with disruptive consequences of change, our fear and self-limiting beliefs will kick into action. You can't escape the fact that change is a disruptor, and it is scary and uncomfortable.

It is, however, our power of choice that allows us to embrace the positive change in our life.

We can control our reaction to the impact that an unexpected event brings to our life, but we cannot control the events of change in our life.

"Life is about choices. Some we regret, some we are proud of. Some will haunt us forever. The message: we are what we chose to be." -- Graham Brown

2. Discover the meaning in life

"Step out of your comfort zone. Comfort zones, where your unrealized dreams are buried, are the enemies of achievement. Leadership begins when you step outside your comfort zone." -- Roy T. Bennett

You will have clarity and focus when you have a sense of purpose and meaning in life. Knowing what is important in your life gives you purpose and sets the direction of how you want to live your life. These elements are particularly important to you in being able to successfully adapt and manage the impact of change in your life.

If you don't have a sense of focus and purpose, you will tend to drift in life. You will also be confined to your comfort zone. With courage and purpose, you will be able to step out of your comfort zone, which will bring about change, and opportunity to learn.

3. Do away with regrets

"The truth is unless you let go, unless you forgive yourself, unless you forgive the situation, unless you realize that the situation is over, you cannot move forward." Steve Maraboll

One of the keys to moving forward in life is letting go of regrets. Regrets have a great impact on your response to change because it is part of the factors that hold you back from doing exploits.

You may miss the opportunities of the present and the future if you are looking back at your past. It is the events of change that bring opportunities in life.

There is no way you can do and undo what has happened in the past, so you should allow bygone to be bygone. You can only choose how you will live in the present. That is the only control you have.

One of the recommended exercises for regret is to blow up some balloons and write regret on each of them. Then release the balloons into the air, and allow them to go, then say goodbye.

Although, it is a quite simple exercise, but it is remarkably effective in dealing with a pile of regrets you have gathered over time.

4. Pen down a list of scary things to do-- then do them

As previously said, change is scary, because it forces people out of their comfort zones. We need to activate our subconscious to get familiar with the unknown and doing scary things. In fact, we should get our subconscious used to doing scary things.

Note down a list of scary things you would like to do but are scared of attempting. It might be the fear of public speaking, fear of heights, fear of engaging in hiking, and so on. Note these things down and start planning on how you will engage in them. After trying them out, you will be surprised at the level of confidence you have developed on a second trial.

5. Pay attention to living a healthy and balanced life

THE PATH TO ACHIEVING YOUR GOAL

"To keep the body in good health is a duty...otherwise we shall not be able to keep the mind strong and clear." -- Buddha

When you are able to balance your health, and your life, you will be able to develop resilience, as well as the ability to handle the disruption that change can bring in your life.

It is normal for stress to show as the normal response to change, or other challenges in our daily life. Stress can help you perform in the long term, in the short term, but constant stress can harm your health.

Therefore, the key to our survival on both physical and emotional levels is finding positive ways to deal with the stress and pressure we face in our daily life.

Actionable Advice

★ The more you resist change, the tougher it gets.

★ We all love the comfort zone. The reason our subconscious likes it is because, it is known, as embracing change means stepping into the unknown, which our subconscious is not in support of.

★ We can control our reaction to the impact that an unexpected event brings to our life, but we cannot control the events of change in our life.

★ Knowing what is important in your life gives you purpose and sets the direction of how you want to live your life.

★ One of the keys to moving forward in life is letting go of regrets. Regrets have a great impact on your response to change because it is part of the factors that hold you back from doing exploits.

"The greatest weapon against stress is our ability to choose one thought over another"
William James

YOU MUST REDUCE YOUR STRESS LEVEL TO BE ABLE TO ACHIEVE YOUR GOALS

How to Conquer Stress

In research conducted by TalentSmart with more than a million people, they found out that in times of stress, 90% of top performers are skilled at managing their emotions to remain calm and in control. They have emotional intelligence.

And the secret to winning the war against stress lies in what you do when you aren't working. And presumably aren't that stressed. Stress has a funny way of sneaking up on you when you least expect it, but how you respond is only half the battle. Otherwise, rather than alleviate it, you fall into bad habits that can magnify your stress.

To control it, contain it, conquer it, you need to fire back in kind, because of stress attacks in all sorts of ways.

Minimization of chores

You need to schedule your chores like you would do anything else during the week. If you don't complete them during the allotted time, you move on and finish them the following weekend. Chores tend to monopolize your free time. And you lose the opportunity to relax and reflect when this happens. You put in a seven-day workweek if you spend all weekend doing them. The worst thing about chores is that a lot of chores feel like work.

Disconnecting yourself from some things

Try to designate specific times on Saturday and Sunday for checking e-mails and responding to voicemails if taking the entire weekend off handling work, e-mails and calls aren't realistic. For instance, schedule short blocks of time will alleviate stress without sacrificing availability. You can check your messages on Saturday afternoon while your kids are getting a haircut and on Sunday evenings after dinner. Because making yourself available to your work 24/7 exposes you to a constant barrage of stressors that prevent you from refocusing and recharging. Disconnecting yourself from some things is the most important strategy. If you can't find a way to remove yourself electronically from your work, then you've never really left work.

Pursuing a passion

Indulging your passions is a great way to escape stress and to open your mind to new ways of thinking. Pursuing things like writing, painting, reading, playing music. If you have kids, playing catch with them can help stimulate different modes of thought that can reap huge dividends over the coming week. When you pursue something, you're passionate about during your time off, you might be surprised what happens.

Scheduling micro-adventures

Studies have shown that anticipating something good to come is a significant part of what makes the activity pleasurable. Knowing that you have something interesting planned for the weekend will not only be fun, come the weekend, but it will significantly improve your mood throughout the week. Plan a hike instead of running on a treadmill. Buy tickets to a play or concert, get reservations for that cool new hotel that just opened downtown. Try something new. Try something you haven't done before or perhaps something you haven't done in a long time.

Get prepared ahead for the upcoming week

When you go into a new week with a plan because all you have to focus on is execution, the week feels more manageable. Thirty minutes of planning ahead of the new week can yield significant gains in productivity and reduced stress. So, the weekend is a great time to spend a few moments planning your upcoming week.

Waking up at the usual time

You end up feeling groggy and tired when you sleep past your regular wake-up time on the weekend. It isn't only disruptive to your day off; it also makes you less productive on Monday because your brain isn't ready to wake up at your regular time. Just go to bed earlier if you need to catch up on sleep. Because it's tempting to sleep in on the weekend to catch up on your sleep. Though it feels nice temporarily, having an inconsistent wake-up time disturbs your circadian rhythm, and can aggravate depression. Your body cycles through an elaborate series of sleep phases for you to wake up rested and refreshed. One of these phases involves preparing your mind to be awake and alert, which is why people often wake up just before their alarm clock goes off, the brain is trained and ready.

Exercising

Innovators and other successful people know that being outdoors often sparked creativity. Getting your body moving for at least 10 minutes releases GABA, a soothing neurotransmitter that reduces stress. You most times have 48 hours every weekend to make it happen. Never say there's no time to exercise during the week. Exercise is a great way to come up with new ideas.

Spending good time with family

If you have kids, take them to the park, take your spouse to his or her favorite restaurant. Pay a visit to your parents. Weekdays are so hectic that the entire week can fly by with little quality family time. Don't allow this to bleed into your weekends. Spending quality time with your family is essential if you want to recharge and relax. Try doing that and you'll be glad you did.

As simple as the tips could look, they are most times not easy to implement when your mind is clouded with stress. But you'll reap the benefits that come with disciplined stress management if you force yourself to attempt the tips provided the next time your head is spinning.

THE PATH TO ACHIEVING YOUR GOAL

> **Actionable Advice**
>
> ★ The secret to winning the war against stress lies in what you do when you aren't working.
>
> ★ Spend quality time with family and friends to reduce stress.
>
> ★ Take exercise seriously.
>
> ★ Don't be caught unawares. Always be prepared.
>
> ★ Indulging your passions is a great way to escape stress and to open your mind to new ways of thinking.

"Balance is feeling derived from being whole and complete; it's a sense of harmony. It is essential to maintaining quality in life and work"
Joshua Osenga

THE PART OF LIFE YOU NEGLECT WILL RETURN WITH ITS CONSEQUENCES

Balancing Your Private and Professional Life

To maintain a healthy equilibrium between personal and professional life is sometimes a big dare and so the work-life stability looks quite tricky.

Provocations arising in personal life affect professional journey and vice versa, and one of those challenges is maintaining equilibrium between personal and professional life. A lot of human beings take such hardships as a burden, yet many enjoy taking up those challenges and fight well to attain better living standards. Life grid has been set up in such a way that it is deficient in absence of challenges. Everyone comes across certain provocations throughout their life span. Life is a challenge that is never easy to face.

Though nature has its way of balancing things. So, every complication has a solution too. But work-life balance is the term used to maintain fluency between personal and professional life. Everyone fights at their levels to get personal and professional life balance depending upon each person's job role and personal statistics. Some medical, etiquette and psychological variations may reflect due to failure in maintaining such essential equilibrium, and in some way, the other affects productivity.

Defining your priorities

You need to define your priorities at the office like at home to be effective and avoid dividing yourself. Nobody has found a way to split themselves into two yet. You cannot be always on all fronts.

When you're at work, ask yourself the tasks that interest you and do them. Know the skills you would like to showcase or develop more. Also, know the projects you would like to involve yourself in. And know the tasks that you could delegate.

In terms of private life, ask yourself, people, you want to spend more time with. Ask yourself if you want to spend more time with your family and friends. Also, if you would like to have the time to cook more often and do the regular activity. Make sure you just define your priorities.

Balancing your private and professional life should become your project and you should work towards its success. It is down to you, do put in all your work to reach your objectives.

Organizing your days

Get yourself to work straight away and make sure you start your day by writing everything that you wish to accomplish. And tick the completed tasks as you go along and at the end of the day it will give you a real feeling of accomplishment. It is imperative to be organized to achieve your objectives. For instance, marking will help you greatly.

One other important is making work timetables a necessity and respect them whatever happens, except in case of emergencies. If you are tired and less productive or if you have finished your tasks for the day, it is not useful to stay just to put in an appearance.

Learn how to delegate tasks

Learn to delegate secondary tasks and focus only on the most important ones. Stop putting yourself on every forefront and wanting to do everything. Identify the tasks which you can delegate and choose competent colleagues with who you can entrust them with. Discuss every aspect of the tasks with them, discuss the objectives, demands, and deadlines. Also, have confidence in them and congratulate them for the works they did.

Learn to say no

Reflect and ask yourself if it is worth it to say yes and put yourself in an impossible situation just to please your boss and colleagues. It is pointless to put yourself under more pressure by accepting new tasks if you already have lots of work. Clearly and honestly explain the situation and the reasons why you can't do a task. You will no longer blame yourself for saying no if you learn to say it with experience, and you will feel a lot better.

Take a lunch break

Leave your workplace or home with colleagues to eat outside, but make sure you don't talk about work worries, go shopping, or do sport. Avoid eating a sandwich quickly in front of your screen and make the most of it by disconnecting from work. The lunch break is a break as its name indicates. In short, take time for yourself.

In this way, you will come back to your job revitalized and ready to work productively all afternoon. This short break is beneficial for your well-being and allows your brain to rest at the same time.

THE PATH TO ACHIEVING YOUR GOAL

Doing physical activities

All activities are beneficial: walking, cycling, doing Zumba, running, swimming, yoga, or meditation allows you to take time for yourself and to eliminate the tensions and pressure felt at the office. To decompress and to make the transition between work and home. Sport is an excellent way to get over the stress of the day. When you spend your whole day seating in front of a computer, it is important to do at least 30 minutes of physical exercise every day.

It is down to you to better organize your time and make the necessary efforts to achieve this. Finding the balance between your personal and professional life is essential for your success and well-being.

How to think outside the box

Thinking outside the box means approaching problems in new or innovative ways. Understanding your position in any particular situation in a way you'd never thought of before and conceptualizing problems differently. It's more than just a business cliché.

It's the ability you cultivate looking at things differently from the way people typically see them. It's the ability you develop to confront problems in ways other than the ways people normally confront problems. You're told to think outside the box all the time, but how exactly do you do that?

Thinking outside the box starts well before you confront a unique situation or problem and start forcing it into a familiar "box" that people already know how to deal with or at least think you know how to deal with.

Make some efforts to push your thoughts up or beyond their limit now and then. You will be able to face a situation that "everybody knows" how to solve if the talents you develop come in handy the next time. Here are some methods of beefing up your out-of-the-box thinking skills.

Simplifying your thoughts

It's easier to take a step back and look at your thoughts, however, if your thoughts can be simplified. You can critique individual thoughts, add to the thoughts, nix the ideas, or expand upon the ideas once you could simplify them. You can't think out of the box when your head is all over the place. Sometimes, you need to stop thinking so much to think outside the box. It can be difficult to remove yourself from what's already inside your head when you become stuck in a tangled web of thoughts and ideas.

Ask yourself why

Ask yourself why you wrote a book if you're writing a book and trying to think outside the box for titles, ask why people should read it, why anyone would want to read it, and why it deserves to be read. Likewise, if you're trying to think of creative ways to sell a product or service, instead of thinking about how to sell to a customer or client, ask yourself why your product or service should be bought. Ask: Why does this matter? Why should anyone care? Why is your product or service unique, why should a customer or client choose you ahead of anyone? When you're trying to think outside the box, ask yourself "why" you're doing what you're doing.

Playing devil's advocate with yourself

Playing devil's advocate with yourself will force you to find flaws or potential loopholes in your ideas and, therefore, propose new ideas or expand on them. Forcing yourself to see the opposite will help you to open your mind to all possibilities. Thinking the exact opposite of what you were already thinking will make you think outside the box. Because it's easy to fall in love with your own words and ideas. After all, you came up with your ideas. However, it's not so easy to refute your thoughts.

Taking new classes or topics

Taking new classes or topics will introduce you to a lot of things you might think you know but never knew. It will expose you to some other aspects of life. It will in turn help you expand both how you look at problems and the breadth of possible solutions you can come up with. Learning a new topic will not only teach you a new set of facts and figures, but it will also teach you a new way of looking at things and making sense of aspects of your everyday life or of the society or natural world you live in.

Working backward

Working backward is just as turning something upside down. And working backward breaks the brain's normal conception of causality. The key to backward planning is, for instance, starting with a goal and think back through the steps needed to reach it until you get to the place you are right now.

Learning about another faith or religion

Starting to see the reason in another religion can also help you develop mental flexibility. You will start to see the limitations of whatever dogma or doxy you follow when you look at all the different ways people comprehend the same mysteries and the fact that they generally manage to survive regardless of what they believe in. It's a revelation that will transfer quite a bit into the non-religious parts of your life.

Learning about how such relations are structured can teach you a lot about how people relate to each other and the world around them. Because religions are the way that humans organize and understand their relationships not only with the supernatural or divine but with each other.

Reading unfamiliar genres of novels

If you read literary fiction, try a mystery or science fiction novel; if you read a lot of hard-boiled detective novels, try a romance; and so on. Don't only pay attention to the story but also to the specific problems the author has to deal with. For example, ask yourself how the fantasy author bypasses your normal skepticism about magic and pull you into their story. Try connecting those problems to the problems you face in your field. For instance, ask a question on how your marketing team might overcome or convince their audience about a new "miracle" product. So, reading is one of the great mental stimulators in our society, but it's easy to get into a rut. Also, try reading something you'd never have touched otherwise.

Seeking advice from a child

You can seek a piece of advice from a child, asking how they might tackle a problem. The idea isn't necessarily about what the child says, but to jog your thinking into a more unconventional path. Understand that children think and speak with ignorance of convention is often helpful. Don't always buy into the notion that children are inherently more creative before society "ruins" them.

> **Actionable Advice**
>
> ★ Balancing your private and professional life should become your project and you should work towards its success.
>
> ★ To tackle stress, first, be clear about your priorities.
>
> ★ You don't have to do everything. Learn to delegate tasks.
>
> ★ Consider looking at challenges from other perspectives.
>
> ★ Always organize your day in advance.

"A growing body of evidence suggests that the single greatest driver of both achievement and well-being is understanding how your daily efforts enhance the lives of others...the definition of a meaningful life are 'connecting and contributing to something beyond the self."
Tom Rath

YOU CAN'T DO MORE THAN WHAT YOU'VE PREPARED YOU BODY FOR

Achieve More by Prioritizing Your Well-being

Few people do argue that mental health should be low on people's priority list. In theory, people know it matters, but then, the reality most times takes over.

A lot of things have taken over people's time. Many have deadlines they must meet up with. Children get sick now and then. And people are too tired. A lot of them get lost in the vortex of their screens.

Many people struggle to place mental health on their never-ending lists, they never mind and keep it at the top despite being in an era being called the "Age of Anxiety" and a "global mental health crisis". The following day calls wake them up again. And they move back to their normal life.

The American Psychological Association reported that people often do not recognize their vulnerabilities to stress and mental health issues or problems until they start showing up with physical health symptoms. This also lines up with the World Health Organization's grim reported that by 2030 stress-related illness will surpass communicable disease.

There is a wide range of activities you can intentionally weave in that science backs as ways to protect and elevate your mental health while you cannot necessarily control the pressures of your modern demands altogether or skirt the inevitable sufferings of life.

Engaging yourself in mindful living

Research showed that you are more likely to thrive when you work to stay in the present moment and avoid the mindless trappings of overwork, technology, and news overload, being stuck ruminating over the past, or locked in anticipatory anxiety over the future. And mindfulness activities such as meditation, deep breathing, and yoga have all been linked to elevated brain chemistry and lower levels of cortisol.

Setting boundaries

Mental health can quickly erode in the face of too many yeses. Decide what's most important, decide to delegate, if necessary. Renegotiate or change your responsibilities. Know well that you can't say yes to everything and still have the time to make mental health a priority.

Finding community

Finding people you can safely and openly share with can help curb self-doubt and provide needed support to navigate the joys and complexities of life. Relationships provide critical protection against loneliness and foster a sense of belonging that human beings are wired for. Loneliness is being called "the new smoking", the health risk of human modern life, where human beings are more connected and disconnected than ever before. Isolation is one thing that can quickly erode mental health.

Breaking up with perfectionism

Expecting perfection and sustaining an inhumane schedule in the long haul can lead you at a greater risk for mental health distress while pursuing rigorous goals can be healthy and lead to positive outcomes. Research has shown that perfectionism can quickly spiral into striving that becomes unhealthy.

Taking daily break rituals

It could be brisk walks, deep breathing, singing in the car, or anything that provides you respite and momentum along the way. Make sure you carve out small chunks of time where you are focused on doing something that renews your mind, body, and soul.

Avoiding consumerism

Research has shown that people will be more inclined to flourish and thrive when they move away from the "goods life" to the "good life", the life that focuses on spending their time and money on lasting things like relationships and legacy. So, the promise of retail therapy, being cool, or having status can lure people into spending money they have on stuff they don't need.

Your mental health is everything. Because without it you can't achieve anything. Your mental health is more important than your job, your grades, status, likes on your feed, and any other metrics of success. There is nothing good about your mental health as the World Health Organization asserts.

THE PATH TO ACHIEVING YOUR GOAL

Actionable Advice

★ Mindfulness activities such as meditation, deep breathing, and yoga have all been linked to elevated brain chemistry and lower levels of cortisol.

★ Understand that you can't say yes to everything and still have the time to make mental health a priority.

★ Finding people you can safely and openly share with can help curb self-doubt and provide needed support to navigate the joys and complexities of life.

★ Research has shown that perfectionism can quickly spiral into striving that becomes unhealthy.

★ Make sure you create some time every day to enable you to focus on doing something that renews your mind, body, and soul.

"Whatever the present moment contains, accept it as if you had chosen it. Always work with it, not against it."
Eckhart Tolle

THE ONLY TIME YOU HAVE IS NOW

Enjoying the Moment with Mindfulness

No matter what you're doing, learning how to be mindful, be more aware of yourself, and your surroundings can help you enjoy the moment. Wherever you are or you may be now, whether you are a working adult or a student, you may feel like life is rushing past you from time to time. Maybe you get swept up in the past, regretting some decision or actions, wishing you had done or said something differently, always learn to be mindful. Because it's most times easy to get distracted with thoughts about what you need to do after work or school, errands you'll need to run, and plans for the weekend.

Always be present in the moment

The only thing you can change is this present, and that starts with being mindful of what you're doing, what is happening around you, and where you are. When you recognize how powerless you are to alter the past or future, it can cause you a lot of stress and anxiety when you get lost in that way of thinking. Worrying about things you can't predict or alter in the future or thinking about how much time you've wasted through the years by dwelling on things you can't change from the past can hinder you from enjoying the moment.

Only observe and look at the things happening around you without judgment. Recognize without judgment that you are temporarily a part of that place. Walk across the ground or sit quietly as you breathe in the air around you. Notice how you fit in with your environment. Focus on concrete, observable sensory information. Try describing any events happening in your immediate environment or your surroundings, in your head. Simply notice them.

Try eliminating distractions

Try scheduling your device usage. When you're trying to enjoy a moment with others or alone, simply turn off your phone or make time for device-free activities. Whether it's a moment spent alone or with others, personal devices like cellphones and tablets can distract you from a moment. Your cellphone or friends' phones can easily ruin the moment when you want to spend quality time with others, or simply sit alone in a calm environment. Because incoming text messages, phone calls, emails, and social media updates or notifications can all distract you from whatever you intend to do. So, you might easily get distracted from enjoying a moment by your electronic devices if you also have countless thoughts running through your head.

Ignoring fleeting thoughts

Imagine each thought that drifts into your mind like clouds floating across the sky. If you do not like a particular thought, simply wait without engaging it and it will slowly pass by and drift away. A pivotal component of mindfulness is accepting your thoughts as they are, without judging them, holding onto them, or resisting them. Remember your thoughts are immaterial. And they only gain meaning when you give them meaning. Also, don't try pushing unpleasant thoughts away, as this may only make your mind dwell on the discomfort of that thought. Don't try grasping at pleasant thoughts. Though It's easy to feel as though your thoughts are in control, especially during a crisis or moments of anxiety. But it's important to remember that you have the power to decide whether or not to engage with a given thought at that moment.

The Important Tips to Living Without Limits

These are clarity, competence, and concentration, and they are key to living without limits:

1. Clarity of Vision, Goals, and Desires

If you are clear about your goals and desire, you will do something every day to accomplish them. Knowing where you are going, and what you want, is what clarity means. This is done by penning down your goals and making plans to accomplishing them. Understand that the little progress you make every day is very essential to achieving your desire, as it will contribute to your self-believe, self-confidence, and make you believe that you can that there is no limit to what you can't achieve.

It is worthy of note that one of the habits of successful people is focusing on their goals every day. The reason is that they tend to regularly focus on their goals and are interested in productivity techniques such as the 80/20 principle. You will stay focused every day if you have clarity of vision and desire.

2. Impeccable competence in your field

It means you are exceptionally good in your chosen field when you develop an impeccable competence in it. You need to submit yourself to learning every day if you want to attain outstanding competence, because growing is also a continuous process, and excellence is a moving target. Using the Pareto principle means you will be concentrating on 20 percent of activities that bring 80 percent results. Therefore, you must commit yourself to doing something in your field every day that will sharpen your competence more, and more.

3. Concentration

Focus and concentration have always been the two key words of success. Concentration is about not being distracted, persevering, and being in tandem with what you want to accomplish, while focusing relates to knowing what you want to do, what you have, and what you want to be. Having the discipline to focus on a single task till it is completed, and not meddle in other things, is what having concentration is all about.

You will begin to think in terms of possibility, and impossibility when you concentrate on doing what you want and becoming excellent in the areas that will make a real difference in your life. When you start dreaming big, you will feel an incredible sense of power and confidence, because you will subconsciously abandon activities that are taking up your time, which will enable you to concentrate your energies on clearing your main constraints.

Lastly, research conducted on the attitude of rich people reveals that 85 percent of them have a big goal that they invest much of their time in every day. If you want to be wealthy, therefore, do what wealthy people do.

Actionable Advice

★ Worrying about things you can't predict or alter in the future or thinking about how much time you've wasted through the years by dwelling on things you can't change from the past can hinder you from enjoying the moment.

★ When you're trying to enjoy a moment with others or alone, simply turn off your phone or make time for device-free activities.

★ If you do not like a particular thought, simply wait without engaging it and it will slowly pass by and drift away.

★ You need clarity of vision, goal, and desire you live without limit.

★ You need to sharpen your saw. Have impeccable competence in your field.

Further reading

Here some recommended resources if you want to look at this topic in greater depth and expand your horizon on setting and achievingyour goals.

Books:

- Brendon Burchard. *High Performance Habits: How Extraordinary People Become That Way*

- Napoleon Hill. *Think and Grow Rich*

- Steve Harvey. *Act Like a Success, Think Like a Success: Discovering Your Gift and the Way to Life's Riches*

FINAL THOUGHTS

If we all want to live a happy, long, and successful life, we need to be proactive about how we manage and face our lives. For us to achieve that success we desire, we need to set goals. Goal setting is just like a compass that leads us to where we would like to see ourselves in the nearest future.

When we talk about goal setting, it is more than just saying what we would like to happen. It is by being deliberate in our actions and taking the necessary steps to actualize them. You will considerably reduce your odds for success if you can't clearly define exactly what you want and understand why you want it in the first place.

It is for this reason that this book is written to help put you through on how you can achieve success in both your personal and professional life. It is advised that you take this book as your goal setting manual, and ensure that you follow all the recommendations, practice the suggested exercises and tips therein. In a couple of months, you will be so glad you did.

Got feedback?

I would love to hear what you think about our book! If you have any suggestions or ideas on how to further improve the book, I would very much appreciate all the feedback that you can give me. Just drop an email to **samuel.jeremy.lucas@gmail.com**.

Also, if you liked the book, and **you would like to leave a public review in Amazon telling us what you liked the most or** how the book has helped you, I would be super grateful for it!

About Samuel J. Lucas

Samuel J. Lucas is a serial entrepreneur, high-performance coach, professional advisor, and associate professor at several business schools.

Samuel has dedicated most of his professional career to creating, advising, and directing companies. However, over the past 12 years he carried out a comprehensive study of the 145 most important books on self-development, happiness, and success.

Over these 12 years, he has also interviewed with hundreds of colleagues, top-notch experts in fields such as personal transformation, leadership, productivity, time management, problem solving, stress management or decision making.

After this life-changing process, he decided to distill all this knowledge, combine it with his extended personal and professional experience, and share it with the world.

Thus, the book series "The secrets to a beautiful life" was born.

Printed in Great Britain
by Amazon